The "Deplorables" and Their Enemies

Beginning with skepticism—in fact, plain lack of interest—the author came to view Donald Trump as the imperfect, at times rough-hewn leader that a desperate American electorate had chosen as their champion. Against what? Against a self-perpetuating Washington bureaucracy and Congress, a metastasizing liberal-left interventionist-welfare state, and a cultural and intellectual elite that held America up to the yardstick of Postmodernist philosophical skepticism, cultural Marxist, and "identity" politics--and found America's founding principles and values of today's middle class contemptible. He realized that the election, for him, had become more a choice between Trump and his enemies than between Trump and Hillary Clinton.

In Donald Trump and His Enemies: How the Media Put Trump in Office, he narrates in real time, with all the drama, conflict, and surprise of the 2016 election, how Trump's brazen, uncompromising candidacy, and his refusal to flinch at any attack on himself or his family, forced American intellectuals on the Left, but especially in the media, to expose their collectivist priorities, willingness to grasp any means to achieve their ends, and hatred for the "deplorables" who, despite it all, elected Donald Trump their standard-bearer.

When You Understand the 2016 Election, You Understand America in A New Way

- *Donald Trump and His Enemies* is being called the book that gets to the bottom of the election: What crucial ideas and values were at stake on the philosophical level in defining what it means to be American?
- Forget every screaming headline about Trump's political incorrectness toward Blacks, Hispanics, women, gays, lesbians, and transgender bathroom advocates—Donway dissects the legends and reveals the reality.
- *Donald Trump and His Enemies* understands the Americans who swept Trump into office with a Republican House and Senate. How they saw through the media dramas of "identity politics." How they resisted the intimidating labels, from "white nationalist" to "deplorables," and asserted their own values on election night--delivering a historic shock to politicians, pundits, and pollsters.
- Walter Donway was among the earliest and most discerningly skeptical advocates of Donald Trump. A veteran of political campaigns since 1960, Donway became a Trump champion because "the media treatment outraged my sense of fair play."
- In real time, from Trump's announcement of candidacy, to his nomination, his election, his violence-lashed inauguration, and the instantaneous "impeach Trump" crusade that greeted the new President, Donway follows the action and coolly dissects the distortions, double-standards, and lies as well as underlying motives of Trump's enemies.
- This is not a breezy read nor a "victory lap." It is excruciating, at times, as the story unfolds, to see near-hysterical attack after attack on Trump's personality—seldom his stands on the issues—as the America media machine focuses on one story: "Get Trump."

- Donald Trump is not a man of theoretical political principles, but he achieved his dreams in America and is a fierce patriot of the America, values, and spirit that made that possible. That assured a head-on crash with the legions of journalists who don't like America as it is, don't like the values of its middle class, and don't admire its spirit.
- This analysis probes down to the philosophical ideas that made possible American civilization and those now seeking to destroy those values. Donway identifies this as a clash of "Modernism" with "Postmodernism."
- It is frightening to see how quickly Trump's enemies, baffled in the battle of ideas, beaten in the election, turned to violence. This is the story of Postmodernism writ large: ideas advanced as self-evident, opposition self-righteously denounced, firm disagreement greeted with violence.
- *Donald Trump and His Enemies* is an education in the dynamics of the election, but also today's urgent issues: global warming ("big climate alarmism," Donway calls it), Bernie Sanders socialism, the $2.0 trillion drag of regulation on the American economy, Obama's gushing visit to *Castro's* Cuba, the public education monopoly's hatred of vouchers—issues that the enemies of Trump tried to sweep aside to talk ceaselessly about "identity politics."
- If you read only one book on the 2016 election, read *Donald Trump and His Enemies.* It bids fair to tell you everything that the mainstream media did not discuss—the truth, the whole truth, and nothing but the truth.

Donald Trump and His Enemies:

How the Media Put Trump in Office

By Walter Donway

Romantic Revolution Books

Donald Trump and His Enemies: How the Media Put Trump in Office

Copyright 2017 © Walter Donway

ISBN-13: 978-1548990640
ISBN-10: 1548990647

Romantic Revolution Books
279 Stephen Hands Path
East Hampton, NY 11937
WDonway@Gmail.com

Also by Walter Donway:

Not Half Free: The Myth That America Is Capitalist by Walter Donway, with a preface by David Kelley. Romantic Revolution Books: New York, 2015.

All his books are available as eBooks or paperbacks on Amazon: https://www.amazon.com/Walter-Donway/e/B00B5H5SA4/ref=ntt_dp_epwbk_0

Dedicated

To Vinay Kolhatkar
Publisher *extraordinaire* of *The Savvy Street*,
Who courageously published it all
While the "mainstream media" went mad with partisan fever

Table of Contents

Introduction

I did not write this book after the election of Donald Trump. As indicated at the end of each chapter, I wrote the chapter as an article—the first one on March 17, 2016—and published it. It was not by hindsight that I reached the conclusion implied by the book's title: that the most significant aspect of the election was the opposition to Trump. This was an observation that grew throughout the nominations, election, and early months of the Trump administration. (The final chapter, not published as an article, I wrote in June 2017).

Although I am keen on political philosophy, and how it manifests in practice, I felt no special interest in the early months of the primaries. None of the candidates excited me. When Trump, late in the process, entered the race for the Republican Presidential nomination, no one could miss the outcry of the media, starting with announcement of his candidacy. I became curious, but I had a problem. I used to joke that I couldn't comment on Trump's ideas because watching him on television gave me hives.

Not quite hives, but watching him made me uncomfortable. I didn't like his loud, emphatic, gesturing, slogan-laden style of speaking and his ceaseless facial expressions. Or his hair. I watched him relatively few times—his nomination acceptance speech and the three debates. I went for information not to television but to reading, first, the "white papers" on the official Trump campaign Web site. Obviously, no candidate, least of all Mr. Trump, researches and writes his own position papers. I found them intelligent and articulate—but you would expect that from a campaign staff.

What drew me in was surprise that Trump's positions tended to be "libertarian." I vote Republican, usually with no enthusiasm, and on the spectrum, I am "libertarian." I am a lifelong devotee of the philosopher and novelist, Ayn Rand, who gave libertarianism an incomparably profound foundation in her philosophy of Objectivism: human nature, reason, ethics, human rights, the voluntary society, and *laissez faire* capitalism under strictly limited constitutional government.

Being Republican, libertarian, and Objectivist, however, did not mean automatic support for Trump. Far from it. Colleagues who shared all my principles early became #NeverTrump; others saw no course but to support the Libertarian Party candidate, Gary Johnson.

I discuss Trump's policy positions many times, here, usually to reiterate that the media seldom did so. But among positions that surprised me were his determination to rein-in the radical environmentalism of the Environmental Protection Agency, slash corporate taxes, and halt proliferation of regulations that now impose a $2.0 trillion annual drag on the U.S. economy. His position in favor of public school "choice" and vouchers also surprised me. These were bound to alienate big voter constituencies. Even his initial explosively controversial proposal for the "wall" can be consistent with libertarianism if the case can be made that the wall is essential to upholding the law.

I wrote a tentative article, the first in this book, imagining an interview with Trump. I had more questions than answers; he abruptly had become "pro-life," a position inconsistent with liberty. His formula for saving or recovering American manufacturing sounded protectionist, a position inconsistent with liberty. In fact, I was still only half serious when I wrote the article. I was dead serious only about violence at his rallies and allegations that he urged on the fights. Introducing violence into the political process is the beginning of the end of the free society. I ended my "interview" with "I will be watching you!"

I followed that theme through the election and its aftermath. There proved to be no basis for fear that Trump's supporters might substitute violence for persuasion. The charge dissolved for want of the slightest substance. Instead, as Trump's enemies faced defeat, and Trump's movement triumphed on November 8, his enemies reverted to the leftist standard: violence in the streets at the inauguration, at airports in response to the temporary suspension of immigration from terrorist-breeding nations, at the University of California , Berkeley, to prevent Trump supporters from speaking, and, as this book is finished, in Hamburg with leftist arson, looting, and attacks on police to protest "capitalism" and Trump's visit.

As Trump's nomination drive gained momentum, I noticed repeated attacks on his lack of experience in public office. At 70, he had been a lifelong businessman and successful in the fierce New York City real estate market; I can think of no U.S. president with a true business resume. Americans have a dismal opinion of their elected representatives—when it comes to Congress, polls indicate support no higher than the *teens*. Rasmussen points out that it rarely has exceeded 20 percent. Washington outsiders have won most Presidential elections since the end of WWII: Dwight Eisenhower, Jimmy Carter, Ronald Reagan, Bill Clinton, and George W. Bush. Barrack Obama essentially was an outsider, too.

Donald Trump was the diametrical opposite of a "career politician." He had no political debts to pay; no political cronies; no favors to repay; and no investment in any legislation or program. He had entered business and made his money like the rest of us. It made me almost giddy to picture this man striding into Washington with *none* of the baggage of the Beltway. And his personal wealth made it unlikely anyone would be "buying" his election for him.

Jettisoning Journalistic, then all, standards

Now, I was following the nomination process in several publications and on online sites for news, commentary, political analysis, and polling results. *Nothing* struck me more forcefully than the partisan, adversarial, relentlessly negative, and increasingly self-righteous, often outright rude treatment of Trump in the mainstream media. It was a vendetta, not journalism.

The claim is not strictly demonstrable, but my sense was that as Trump topped off the votes needed for nomination, the tenor of media coverage changed. The pattern became that the Democratic Presidential nominee, Hillary Clinton, and the mainstream media, worked synergistically to batter Trump. The Clinton campaign staff, which, for more than a year, had been researching and collecting all possible scandals about her potential opponents, now began to release these stories at pivotal points—for example, the day before a television debate and, once, during a debate.

The media then "covered" the story, elaborating it, editorializing about it, holding breathlessly indignant panel discussions, interviewing Hollywood stars for their reactions. They literally filled media space, or on-air time, with anti-Trump commentary.

The highest impact, of course, was achieved by supposed revelations about Trump's character, behavior, and attitudes. Almost all involved "identity politics" (the significance of this will be discussed):

■   The Trump University court case and Trump's statement that a judge of Mexican-American origin should recuse himself.

■   A case, going back several decades, in which the Trump real-estate empire was charged with several instances of racial discrimination in renting apartments.

■   The "pussy tapes" story.

■   The "fat shaming" story.

■   The "mocking a disabled reporter" story.

These stories dominated media coverage of the election, positioning Trump as the politically incorrect, bigoted threat to racial, ethnic, sexual, and other groups. Hillary Clinton spoke daily of "all of us," "all Americans," and repeated pledges to every conceivably "exploited group" that government, at last, would come to its aid with new programs. I investigated these damning allegations. I did not do it alone; I could not. There were online sites deep in the shadows of the mainstream media where writers did their homework. One by one, I discovered that these stories were false, greatly exaggerated, presented out of context, or rested upon a blatant double standard. You will judge for yourself the validity of my interpretations.

The focus of my articles became the campaign of defamation conducted by the mainstream media to stop Trump. By the end, the media had tossed aside objectivity, factuality, fairness, and—at last—decency in the race to destroy its target. What arrested my attention was that through all these attacks voter support for Trump never wavered. It appeared to solidify and increase.

I saw this in polls, of course, but also on Facebook, Linked-in, and Twitter. Posts and commentary of Trump backers on social media turned almost exclusively to questioning, rebutting, deploring, and ridiculing the media. Perhaps it was inevitable; all the mainstream media would countenance was attacks on Trump. What else for voters to discuss? My rebuttals of the "scandal" attacks on Trump were "shared" on social media by hundreds of contacts, reaching thousands of readers.

By the end of the election season, anyone awake knew Trump had *given up* on the mainstream media. In a move his enemies loathed, this 70-year-old man turned to the latest "hot" technology, Twitter, mastered it, and used it brilliantly to bypass the media. CNN reported that Trump could reach 27 million followers on his personal Twitter account (today, he reaches another 16 million on his #POTUS official Presidential account). If the press released a new horror tale for the evening news, his staff did not have to write a press release and wait for the press to pick it up the next day--after the attack had gained momentum. A decoy popped into the air and Trump blasted it.

The divorce

When the election came, the media thought they had won, that Trump was out, Clinton in. That hubris waxed right up to election eve as commentators on every channel awaited returns from polling places and prepared for a well-earned, gleeful triumph. Trump? He was doing what he did best: traveling the country, often making five speeches a day, bypassing the media to speak to "his people." The press, I recall, minimized this tireless determination by describing him as "a lonely man" wandering the boondocks, still hoping. In fact, he was in states such as Wisconsin and Michigan, drawing crowds, and preparing to take electoral votes deemed safe for Clinton.

The media mantra had been: How could any decent, intelligent person support Trump? What must they be *thinking*? And the media told them what they were "thinking" by characterizing their candidate as racist, xenophobic, sexist, misogynist, anti-Semitic, insensitive to the disabled, insensitive to the bathroom preferences of transgendered individuals, and standing for nothing but white nationalist desire to build "the wall" and wreck health care for the poor.

Who could *support* this man? People who were...well, reread the above characterization of Trump. How could supporters of Trump and enemies of Trump live together in the same country? My wife of 20 years told me that she didn't think she could continue to live with someone who supported Trump. She told her relatives (my in-laws) that I might protest the ugly election by not voting or voting for the libertarian candidate. I let it go because I had no slightest hope of communicating with Trump haters. Or they with me. We had been taught this by the mainstream media. Thus, personal relations among relatives, friends, and colleagues were collateral damage in the media war to obliterate Trump.

The bright red fire

On election night, I sat home watching the returns on PBS-TV. My wife had decided to watch the election "with friends." Not with an enemy. As the evening went on, beginning with an assumed 100-plus Clinton electoral votes from the heavily populated bi-coastal states such as California, New York, and Pennsylvania, commentators finally noticed, with rising alarm, that a bright red fire was burning across the American heartland.

It started with the Florida upset—the end of "stop Trump early" hopes—and crossed middle America east of Mississippi. To the horror of the commentators, the red fire burned north into states assumed to be for Clinton.

Around midnight, nothing remained for the media but a few fading hopes. When Pennsylvania appeared to go for Trump, it was over. "No one," even most Trump supporters, could quite believe it. The PBS commentators expressed shock, chagrin, and even a quiver of humility. Why were we all *wrong*? How did all the polls get it *wrong* even on the last day? How did we *miss* what was happening in the "other America"? How did this catastrophe *happen*?

CNN wrote, the morning after the election:

The polls were wrong. Projection models were wrong. Veterans of previous presidential campaigns were wrong. Trump's victory is one of the most stunning upsets in American political history. American voters swept Republicans into power, handing the GOP the White House, the Senate and the House in a wave that no one saw coming.

For a day or two, some publications, including the *New York Times*, made a show of soul-searching. We must change, listen to more voices. That sort of thing. Six months or more after the election, the *Times* is running big ads about their "search for truth," "hard truth," "the facts," "the real story." What do you suppose they doth protest too much? They have introduced a few small features to present "other voices." I am available as a columnist.

My article summing up the election zeroed-in on what I call the "Postmodern media," how it staged the election, and how it failed. The media's humiliation and rage were palpable. They got behind the immediate drive to invalidate the vote; they ran articles blaming the "fake news" on the "uncontrolled" social media; they attacked Trump as a Twitter "troll" and compared him in one article with the Nazis.

My articles following the election, on the inauguration, and on the first months of the new administration are included. They carry forward the story, the media's new goal of reversing the election, and public reaction to Trump's first decisions as President.

What I grasped as I put together this book, reviewing chapters written in "real time," is that this election was not about Trump versus Clinton. It was about *"Trump and his enemies"* in the media. The partisan media crusade and how Trump countered it, going directly to his supporters, is part of this story. The media dropped all pretense of neutrality, dropped objectivity, jettisoned truth, and, finally, flung aside decency and seethed with indignation at the politically incorrect Republican candidate. Trump's middle American supporters rejected that *entire framework* of judgment. They rejected *identity politics* as *the* issue in the campaign. And they experienced the attack on Trump as an attack on their values and worldview. It was obvious to them that the media deemed them "deplorables." On election day, they voted their values and worldview—their answer to Trump's enemies, who had become their enemies, too.

I will offer those who opposed President Trump, and are working to "stop" him, "resist" and find a way to impeach him, some advice. If the attacks on Trump continue, the 24/7 crusade to overturn the election, then Trump will win re-election in 2020 *no matter what* his record in office. Because his supporters will ask how *any* man, however valiant, could accomplish his goals under these conditions— and they will be right. Trump will be their champion just for having survived four years of nonstop hostility in Washington, DC, which cast a preposterous 90.9 percent of its votes for Hillary Clinton and 4.2 percent for the new President of the United States.

I suggest that the reader, at this point, has a choice. I have set the scene, now, for my story. A reader now can go straight to chapter 1. What I do in the remainder of this introduction is 1) explain some key terms I use, such as "mainstream media" and "liberal left," and 2) summarize a philosophical theory that appears throughout the book: the philosophy of Postmodernism. It is explained over the course of the book, also but here I present it in one place. The choice is the reader's.

Coming to terms: "mainstream media" and "liberal-left"

Whether you are an unrepentant Trump voter (why *should* you repent?) or are still recovering from indignation at, and anger at, and perhaps fear of the America that elected this 45th President (how can you occupy the same country?), I want to persuade you of one thing: You cannot understand the red wildfire that burned across "middle America" on November 8, 2016—stunning pollsters, pundits, politicians, and plain people—without grasping the role of what is called the "mainstream media."

Lest I be accused of sweeping generalization, or a smear, let me be specific. By "mainstream media," I refer to those historic journalistic names—the *New York Times, Washington Post, L.A. Times, Chicago Tribute*—those ubiquitous TV networks and shows—*CNN, PBS, CBS, NBC,* and *MSNBC* and "Washington Week" and its legion of imitators—and those prestigious periodicals of public opinion—the *New Yorker, Atlantic, Harper's, Economist*, and others. Today, they should be characterized as the "liberal-left" media.

That oft-resented hyphenated label is necessary because today the term "liberal" retains no hint of the original Nineteenth Century concept, which meant advocating "liberty" from government taxation, regulation, and control in favor of the individual's freedom. Today, "liberalism," sometimes called "progressivism," denotes advocacy of the interventionist/welfare state: steadily increasing government power, intervention, and regulation in every sphere of life—exactly the opposite of what "liberalism" once meant. Thus, the explanatory hyphenation, which adds "left" to the description. In America, today, "liberalism" stands for "socialism"—specifically, as *New York Times* columnist Paul Krugman explains, European "democratic socialism." That, in turn, is the promise that government will intervene to control property, production, trade, social relations, education, the environment, and health care without revolutionary violence--without either communism or national socialism-because it will be done by vote. If a majority of your countrymen vote to confiscate your property and regulate your life, that is "democratic" (true) and socialist (true). But it is the opposite of liberty.

Both major political parties in the United States, our university and college faculties, and the "mainstream media" are "liberal-left," "social democratic." They energized the challenge candidacy of Sen. Bernard Sanders and were his chief supporters. Thank you, there will be no more questions on this.

The three-way race: candidates, voters, media

In the 2016 U.S elections--the race for President and seats in Congress and state governments--the candidates and voters were only *two* of the participants. When Hillary Clinton and Donald Trump traveled the country to meet voters and speak to them directly—a vital, colorful American tradition—those two participants communicated directly. But for most Americans, all day and evening, and for the watching world, the election was what the mainstream media *said* it was.

Once the favorite of the media, Sen. Sanders, the only avowed "socialist" in the U.S. Senate, had been defeated by Hillary Clinton, the entire focus of the media turned to electing her. She was the obvious choice of the liberal-left. But, far more, she was the choice of the *Postmodernist* media—and that is a crucial theme of this book.

The media stages the first postmodernism election

I am insisting that to understand the election you must understand the role of media. And that you *cannot understand* without knowing that intellectuals in every realm of American life are knowing or unknowing converts to the philosophy of Postmodernism.

All political systems, principles, and concepts emerge from an underlying philosophy. Since the Greek philosophers such as Plato and Aristotle politics has been treated as a formal branch of philosophy, derived from its positions on the nature of reality, the nature of man and his means of knowledge, the nature of the good (morality or ethics), and the nature of human society.

Plato's view of real knowledge as insight or intuition into a special metaphysical realm, insight achieved only after years of rigorous training, implied government by experts--"philosopher kings." Aristotle's non-mystical, naturalistic theory of the senses and reason implied participation in government by all adult men. (His theory of the nature of women, like the views of virtually all Greek philosophers, excluded women from participation.) The underlying premises dictate the politics. This has held true of every political system since the birth of philosophy in ancient Athens.

The American political system, as defined in the *Declaration of Independence* and the *U.S. Constitution*, and in more depth in *The Federalist Papers* and writings of the founders, like Thomas Jefferson, emerges explicitly from the philosophy of the British and French Enlightenment and Age of Reason. The philosophical premises underlying the system are that all humans are endowed by nature with reason and able to understand the world and guide their own actions. Because reason is an attribute of the individual, and his means of survival, he must be left free to exercise his judgment (the basis of "rights"), and allow others to do the same. The role of government is to protect him in this free exercise of reason, and the actions it dictates, in every area of life. Thus rights, freedom in all areas of life, equality as a citizen, the rule of law, and strict limits on the role and powers of government define the American experiment.

These principles did not initially shape all American politics. It took half-a-century to eradicate the hideous contradiction posed by human slavery and longer still to recognize the full political equality of women. But the principles defined the structure, dictated the course, and protected the integrity of the American experience for some 250 years and counting.

The final link in my explanation is as follows. In Europe, the philosophy of the Enlightenment, known today as "Modernism," was challenged, rejected, and replaced by a philosophy originating in Germany beginning with the work of Immanuel Kant (1724-1804) and his peers, but elaborated by his many successors such as Hegel, Schopenhauer, and Nietzsche. German "idealism" rejected all essential philosophical premises of the Enlightenment: a knowable reality, the efficacy of reason, the ability of the individual to understand the world, the importance of the individual versus the collective. The result of the rejection Modernism and rise of Postmodernism was emergence in Nineteenth Century Europe of new forms of government, predominantly socialism in the form either of Marxist communism or German national socialism (Nazism).

Postmodernism, as German idealism and its offspring came to be called, began to work its way into American universities in the Nineteenth Century and, in many variations, extensions, and modifications today dominates higher education in the humanities and social sciences. In America, Britain, France, and other countries with governments firmly rooted in Enlightenment Modernism, Postmodernism did not have the disastrous consequences for government suffered by Russia, Germany, and Italy. But now, Postmodernism dominates American intellectual life, including philosophy, and will work out its logic in society, politics, and every other area of life.

Here is how Prof. Stephen R. C. Hicks of Rockford University, author of the best critique of Postmodernism, *Explaining Postmodernism: Skepticism and Socialism from Rousseau to Foucault*, characterizes the face of Postmodernism in America today:

Postmodernism became the leading intellectual movement in the late twentieth century. It has replaced modernism, the philosophy of the Enlightenment. For modernism's principles of objective reality, reason, and individualism, it has substituted its own precepts of relative feeling, social construction, and group-ism. This substitution has now spread to major cultural institutions such as education, journalism, and the law, where it manifests itself as race and gender politics, advocacy journalism, political correctness, multiculturalism, and the rejection of science and technology.

For the view of a scientist, here is Prof. Steven Pinker, then director the Center for Cognitive Neuroscience at the Massachusetts Institute of Technology, now Professor of Psychology at Harvard University, in his 1997 book, *How the Mind Works*:

Many of us have been puzzled by the takeover of humanities departments by the doctrines of postmodernism...according to which objectivity is impossible, meaning is self-contradictory, and reality is socially constructed. The motives become clear when we consider statements like 'Humans have constructed and used gender—human beings can deconstruct and stop using gender,' and "The heterosexual/homosexual binary is not in nature, but is socially constructed, and therefore deconstructable.

In my words, not Pinker's, *objectivity, meaning, and reality are denied so that no one can tell me that my wishes, hopes, and whims are not reality.* What is "deconstructed," in fact, is our means of knowing and acting in reality. The Postmodernist seeks power over "social reality"— other people—by disarming them intellectually and morally.

Why Postmodernism lost the election—this time

So far, Americans, except perhaps in "media capitals" on both coasts, have not absorbed Postmodernism. That is why "middle American" Trump supporters butted heads with the media. But recent generations of reporters, commentators, and writers, like others in the world of ideas, attended colleges where, for the most part, the humanities and social sciences are dominated by Postmodernism. This is especially true of the "elite" institutions--the Ivy League colleges on the East coast and the great public universities on the West coast. Their graduates hold key positions throughout the media.

This book discusses how these reporters, editors, and commentators viewed the rise of Donald Trump from the perspective of Postmodernism, including liberal-leftism, and became his "enemies." They responded with "advocacy journalism," shaped by the premise that there are no objectively right and wrong ideas and that *neutrality is impossible* because everyone sees ideas only through the lens of his or her race, sex, and economic class. Every story given 24/7 coverage had to do with alleged racism, sexism, wealth—with the poor, the black, women, immigrants, gays and lesbians, "white" nationalists— with discrimination, insensitivity, disrespect, cruelty, and selfishness. This is the philosophy of Postmodernism that tried to define the terms of the election.

It failed because Trump appealed to Americans not college educated (as the media *tirelessly* reminded us), or educated in traditionalist or religious colleges, or too old to have been indoctrinated in college. These Americans and the media could not comprehend each other because they have different philosophical premises. Americans still viewing life in the framework of Modernism—historic American principles, values, and perspectives—heard the words of the media. But they did not share the philosophical context, value context, that determined the exclusive emphasis of the media on identity politics and the vehemence of personal attacks on Trump. They *did* know that their values were under assault, scorned, derided, and stamped "deplorable."

And they didn't like it.

Chapter 1

I Need an Interview with Donald Trump

Donald J. Trump is becoming significant. He is racking up a roster of delegates to the Republican nominating convention that leaves friends and foes convinced—with glee or gibbering fear, respectively—that he might "lock up" the convention. Then, we would be deciding whether to vote for Mr. Trump versus Hillary Clinton or Bernard Sanders. He is significant because he has defied a hostile, now nigh-hysterical, media and prevailed—as Barry Goldwater, for example, could not—and, in fact, garnered an estimated $1.6 billion in free publicity. Critics groan that the intensive media assault has been a big gift to Mr. Trump, whose campaign so far has had to spend almost zilch on advertising. Mr. Trump, as few Republican candidates before him, has reached—shouted—over the heads of the media to speak to "the people."

There is no candidate for U.S. President that I have felt a more urgent need to meet. That is not going to happen, but I say it because I agree with many of his positions, at least as broadly stated; can understand his abrasive politically incorrect defiance; but believe everything most important about him lies in his "true" motivations. I believe that half-anhour with the man could clarify what an eon of quotations and campaignstop performances cannot.

But first, let me briefly and without comment list some positions he has taken in this campaign or in the past that I find appealing. For this, I rely on a useful site called "On the Issues.org."

■ Cut the entire Environmental Protection Agency and Department of Education.

■ Black lives matter, but we need a strong police presence; police are the most mistreated people in America.

■ Climate change is a hoax.

■ Oil is this country's lifeblood.

■ When you love America, you protect it with no apologies.

■ Better to have Middle East strongmen than Middle East chaos.

■ Get rid of the regulations that are destroying us.

■ Replace ObamaCare with health savings accounts.

■ ObamaCare is a catastrophe that must be repealed and replaced.

■ Kill ObamaCare before it becomes a trillion-ton weight.

■ Don't raise the minimum wage, it makes us non-competitive.

■ Full and unequivocal support for the Second Amendment.

Frankly, Donald…

And now, my conversation with Mr. Trump.

Mr. Trump—may I call you, "Donald?" In December 1999, you stated unequivocally that you supported a woman's right to choose an abortion, perhaps with certain limitations. In 2011, when you became seriously engaged in Presidential politics, you said: "I am now pro-life, after years of being pro-choice."

On the campaign trail, today, you say "abortions must stop." You compare yourself in making this journey with Ronald Reagan. To me, your complete reversal might be plausible for a man in his thirties, coming to terms with life, but in a man almost 70, married three times, and easy with the lifestyle of the casino, this pro-life awakening just when you entered politics is troubling.

Donald, lean forward, now, so I can ask you this in utter confidence. You were a declared Democrat in 2004, making large contributions to Hillary Clinton's campaign, and supporting a woman's right to choose an abortion. In 2016, you are a Republican, stating that you are pro-life. I am aware that *no* individual seeking the Republican nomination has any chance to succeed as a supporter of a woman's right to choose an abortion; the dominance of the evangelicals at the nomination stage is decisive.

And so, I would like to know—lean closer—do you pay lip service to pro-life as the unavoidable cost of the Republican nomination? And do you intend, in office, once again to emulate Ronald Reagan, who as president did nothing to limit a woman's choice?

Thank you, Donald, I will keep your reply strictly confidential.

Mexico

Next, Donald, about the Mexican thieves, rapists, and drug dealers pouring across the border into the United States. You mentioned them in your speech in June 2015 at Trump Tower in New York City announcing your candidacy for the nomination. Given the importance of that speech, and ample time to prepare, your remarks do not get a pass as "just Donald spouting' what he really believes, straight from him to you.

No one as politically astute as you, and as aware of the forces of political correctness, could have failed to know that you would be launching your campaign right into a Force Ten storm of criticism. You seemed to be declaring yourself, from the start, as the "anti-immigration president"—not to mention the bigoted President. And arguably, this has been the bedrock of your "populist popularity."

But, as the storm reached full force, you did offer an explanation— and an excuse. You said you were referring only to that group of illegal immigrants dumped on our side of the border by the Mexican government in seeking to rid itself of criminals—not to illegal Mexican immigrants in general.

I find it interesting that a reading of your remarks supports the possibility of that interpretation. You said: "When Mexico sends its people, they're not sending their best... They're sending people that have lots of problems, and they're bringing those problems with [them]. They're bringing drugs. They're bringing crime. They're rapists. And some, I assume, are good people."

It is an odd formulation to say, if referring to the entire diverse horde of illegal immigrants coming across the border day and night, that "Mexico sends..." these people. So perhaps, after all, you were referring to the Mexican government; but you did not specify how the Mexican government might achieve this transfer of criminals.

At the same time, you proposed what is being criticized as kind of Berlin Wall, or Great Wall of America, to seal our border with Mexico. Today, there already, according to *Wikipedia,* is a border fence 580 miles long on a U.S.-Mexico continental land border that is 1,954 miles. That means that roughly 25 percent of the wall you propose has been built, much of it during the Obama administration.

In other words, the heart of your proposal for dealing with illegal immigration—the wall—could be presented quite conservatively. Complete the remaining 70 percent of the wall, which, as we speak, is still being done in Texas. Complete it because every nation must control its border, and every nation does exert such control. More than 200,000 Mexicans a year cross the border illegally; 85,000 succeed in entering our country. So, does a flood of drugs from Latin and South America and the gangsters who run them.

Donald, all I am saying here is that you did not need to make this among the most inflammatory issues on the campaign trail, today. You did not need to do so. You chose to do so.

Tell me why I should not conclude that you decided deliberately to arouse populist anger, fear, and hatred toward immigrants, illegal and legal, because this has fueled your campaign.

I see. Well, thank you for that attempt at a clarification, Donald.

Have you read about the rise of violence as the chief political tactic in the German Weimar Republic as the insurgent Nazis, Communists, and others created cadres to beat up protestors and, eventually, to conduct fullscale clashes against each other in the streets? I don't see you in that context, but you are rapidly handing evidence to your critics that along with deliberately incendiary rhetoric, and choice of issues that turn groups against each other, you are using that anger you have evoked to silence opposition without the need to persuade.

Growing the U.S. Economy

Next, Donald, about making America great again, growing the U.S. economy at six percent a year, making the economy dynamic, and bringing jobs back from Japan, China, and Mexico.

How will you do that? In 2016, as far as I can see, you put forward a single specific proposal: keep corporations from moving parts of their operations abroad and "bring corporations home" along with money they have abroad. As a corollary, "bring jobs home" from lower-cost manufacturing countries like China and Mexico. Both trends that you would reverse have been underway and strengthening for decades. You do not, however, say how you would change things.

That is different from 2011, when you did make a powerful, dramatic proposal to eliminate the corporate income tax. You said, then, it was about the highest in the world and asked how we expected corporations to remain in America, or return, if we taxed them at 39 percent of profits. I see nowhere that you have repeated that proposal in the current campaign.

You see, Donald, you propose to transform the U.S. economy toward huge economic growth, effective manufacturing competition with China, and revival of jobs America has been losing for years. Could you just tell me, confidentially, how?

You referred once, I think, to eliminating regulations that "are killing us." You referred once to limiting government's role to public works, public safety, and little else. You proposed, once, to eliminate the Environmental Protection Agency. You said fight crony capitalism with a level playing field. Each of these proposals, in principle, if carried out, might have the potential for truly reviving American enterprise. All now lie in the past, unmentioned in this campaign.

Well, that uses up my half hour, Donald. I think that at our next meeting I would like to explore how you feel about violence as a political tactic. I realize that the media's focus on this aspect of your campaign, as on many others, represents at least in part a frantic search for means to discredit you. I mean where were their moans about introducing violence into the political equation when protestors went on a rampage over "police killings"? And I have no doubt there is pushing, shoving, poster tearing, and other intimidation at the rallies of other candidates.

Problem is, Donald, that you stand up there behind the security cordon and say, "Go for'em," "Give'em one for me," and then explain that these are expressions of "love for America." Then, you seem to crow that all the protestors have been scared away.

Believe me, Donald, I am old enough to recall how the media portrayed the 1964 Republican nominee, Barry Goldwater, whose *laissez faire* capitalist views and case for limited government had been stated in the U.S. Senate for years, and eloquently and often in print, as a fascist. When I read such attacks on you, my first inclination is to dismiss them as mud-slinging.

I will be watching you.

Published March 17, 2016, in *The Savvy Street*.

[Editorial note: This book is about the election of President Trump. But it also is about my "conversion," at first, tentative, then increasingly firm, to Trump partisanship. Chapters 2 and 3 address the second theme, not the first. These stories, which I wrote in "real time" about President Obama and Democratic Presidential candidate Sanders, "interrupt" the Trump story to illustrate how other developments—the Obama Cuba gambit and the Sanders "one percent" saga—helped to put Trump's candidacy into perspective.]

Chapter 2

Barack Obama's Last Hurrah: "¡*Viva Cuba Communista!*"

On Monday, U.S. President Barack Obama, with his wife and two daughters, began a state visit to communist Cuba, and spoke that afternoon to the people of Cuba—standing beside Cuban dictator Raul Castro, a declared communist for more than half a century, who was awarded the Soviet Union's Order of Lenin.

Novelist and philosopher Ayn Rand was a refugee to America after the murderous Bolshevik communist takeover of 1917, in Russia, which extinguished the few months of freedom that followed the overthrow of the Czar by the forces of liberation. It was from Russia's first free democratically elected government that Lenin and the Bolshevik cadres seized power.

Ayn Rand incisively identified "dictatorship" by four characteristics.

Political Prisoners

The first is imprisonment or execution without trial for "political" crimes. The organization Human Rights Watch (HRW) reported in "World Report 2015: Cuba":

"In December 2014, President Barack Obama announced that the United States would normalize diplomatic relations with Cuba and ease restrictions on travel and commerce with the island in exchange for several concessions by the Cuban government, including a commitment to release 53 political prisoners...

"The Cuban Commission for Human Rights and National Reconciliation (CCDHRN)—an independent human-rights group the Cuban government views as illegal—received over 7,188 reports of arbitrary detentions from January through August 2014..."

In exchange for the less-than-convincing change of heart on political prisoners, Mr. Obama gives Cuba full diplomatic recognition. Opens full trade. Clears the way for a flood of tourism. And takes his family there so that in a talk to the Cuban people he can comment on the wonderful history, the great scenery, and, yes, the great food in Cuba. Today, in Cuba, private restaurants are permitted only 12 patrons at a time and must employ only family members.

One-Party Rule

The next characteristic of dictatorship is one-party rule. Not much argument, here; there has not been an election or any other political party but the Communist Party in Cuba since Fidel Castro, his brother Raul Castro, and the executioner Che Guevara, came out of the Sierra Madre mountains in 1959 to seize power from the government of Fulgencio Batista, who had fled. HRW does not bother to mention elections because there simply are none.

Property Rights

The next characteristic is denial of property rights. Raul Castro supposedly has been struggling with this since Fidel Castro became ill and Raul Castro became head of the Cuban Communist Party and assumed all positions of power. In the *2016 Index of Economic Freedom,* Cuba ranks dead last in the entire region of Central and South America and the Caribbean.

But, in 2008, Mr. Castro hinted that cell phones might become legal. Also, DVDs and microwaves. Maybe. Monthly wages in Cuba remain at an average of 20 U.S. dollars. It really is laughable, or tragic, to know that there was widespread starvation in Cuba's "special period" (1989-1993) of famine when the Soviet Union collapsed and Cuba lost its huge subsidies.

For a brief overall statement from *Countries of the World*, Cuba Index 2017:

"The Cuban government has slowly and incrementally implemented limited economic reforms, including allowing Cubans to buy electronic appliances and cell phones, stay in hotels, and buy and sell used cars. The Cuban government also opened some retail services to 'self-employment'... Recent moves include permitting the private ownership and sale of real estate and new vehicles, allowing private farmers to sell agricultural goods directly to hotels, and expanding categories of self-employment."

Freedom of Speech and Press

The single most defining feature of dictatorship is suppression of freedom of speech and press. If that freedom exists, a country's citizens do not face government force with no recourse; they can speak out, write, and publish. No dictatorship, however, can tolerate or survive such freedom—and none ever has.

Here is HRW on freedom of expression in Cuba:

"The government controls all media outlets in Cuba and tightly restricts access to outside information, severely limiting the right to freedom of expression. Only a very small fraction of Cubans can read independent websites and blogs because of the high cost of, and limited access to, the Internet. While people in cities like Havana, Santiago de Cuba, or Santa Clara have access to the Internet, people in more rural areas are not able to go online.

"A May 2013 government decree directed at expanding Internet access stipulates that the Internet cannot be used for activities that undermine 'public security, the integrity, the economy, independence, and national security' of Cuba—broadly worded conditions that could be used against government critics...."

Cuba is a full-fledged dictatorship, a vicious anachronism in our time, ruled by a man who became a revolutionary at the height of the

Cold War in the days of Joseph Stalin and for more than half a century, through collapse and disappearance of the Soviet Empire, the movement of the People's Republic of China to a partial market economy, has dutifully enforced one of the few remaining socialist dictatorships in the world.

President Obama not only "opened" Cuba, which could have been done by formally upgrading our embassy and conceding some trade openings, he swept into Cuba with declarations of friendship and crucial mutual interests between the countries. He formally, but also personally, with a blaze of publicity, summoned American tourists to flood into Cuba.

Tourism has become critical to survival of the Cuban economy, which has stagnated, crushed by state control and regulation, permanently stunted by the escape to America of thousands of the most able Cubans, and crippled as Cuba's one big crop, sugar, has been collapsing in price on international markets. But as Americans now swarm into Cuba, the dictatorship keeps its grasp on which Cubans may leave the country—no human right advocates, for example; which Cuban-Americans may come to visit—no political critics; and who can move within the country. Within the country, there is a desperate desire to move from rural areas to the big cities because socialist agriculture has led to near starvation. More pointedly, the government prevents dissidents from coming to the capital city for meetings.

The Better Castro?

Only in contrast to his brother, Fidel, a mentality shaped by nothing but power lust, a mind frozen for half-a-century in Marxist ideology, impervious to any change, any fact—even, apparently, cell phones and DVDs—is Raul Castro more "liberal."

And yet, if there has been a "formative" experience in Raul Castro's life, it has been the astonishing shock of the collapse of the Soviet Union; he was Cuba's liaison to the Soviet secret police (KGB) as early as 1953, and for years afterward. He knows that a dictatorship with absolute power over its people can collapse overnight. The only chance for survival of the Cuban communist dictatorship is tourism, which is now Cuba's single greatest hope for new income. Even now, remittances to Cuban families from Cubans living in the United States is a mainstay against collapse.

In his speech today, in which Mr. Obama repeatedly did obeisance to the Castro brothers, he mentioned, in the most general terms, "human rights." He said that the future of Cuba would be decided by Cubans, no one else. He should have specified he meant not one, two, or a dozen Cubans would make that decision, as they have for half a century, but the Cuban people at large. He said:

"At the same time, as we do wherever we go around the world, I made it clear that the United States will continue to speak up on behalf of democracy, including the right of the Cuban people to decide their own future. We'll speak out on behalf of universal human rights, including freedom of speech and assembly and religion. Indeed, I look forward to meeting with and hearing from Cuban civil society leaders tomorrow." Mr. Obama did not mention the almost-bizarre control of property rights to the point where the computer, internet, and cell phone revolution—today's most crucial individual-to-individual global communication—are virtually nonexistent in Cuba. But the American press, cheerleading the visit, made much of the fact that one—one— internet café now would open in Havana.

Mr. Obama did not mention the arrest of political protestors, including arrests immediately before he arrived. He did not mention the thousands of Cuban political dissidents beaten, tortured, dying in Cuba prisons (*World Report 2015*: Cuba).

Mr. Obama said that in the future the Cuban people would decide their own future democratically. He did not say that this necessitates the end of the half-century monopoly of the Communist Party of Cuba.

He mentioned freedom of speech, the essence of freedom, but coupled it with freedom of religion. Then, saying no more about freedom of speech, he went into detail about freedom of religion and the Cuban Catholic Church. Raul Castro, born Catholic, educated in Jesuit schools, now in his mid-eighties, has said he will return to the Catholic Church. Perhaps, thus, he can avoid going to hell for his crimes, which began with the mass execution of Cuban soldiers when he and brother Fidel seized power.

Defending Human Rights. Mr. Obama Attacks...Sex Trafficking

Mr. Obama said that Raul Castro has agreed to welcome human rights groups into Cuba. For what? To deal with human sex trafficking, "which we agree is a profound violation of human rights." At last, a human right upon which the United States and Cuba can agree—the right not to be a sex slave.

The opening of American-Cuban relations could have been handled far better. It could have been cast in realistic terms. The chief thing would be opening Cuba to American tourism and investment. That is what Raul Castro needs.

As Americans in thousands flood into Cuba, there is no possibility that the dictatorship will keep the lid on freer discussion, movement of publications, opening of the internet and cell phone traffic, and the flow of news between the two countries. The only recourse of the Cuban authorities—arrests of tourists, repression of their activities—will be impossible.

I am certain that Raul Castro knows that. And I entertain a fond hope—perhaps no more than that—that this is what he seeks as his fanatical, doctrinaire, murderous brother, 90 this August, nears death. Raul Castro always has been a quiet, efficient, undemonstrative man, not given to the rhetoric of propaganda and ideology.

Perhaps he will play Mikhail Gorbachev in Cuba, proposing to introduce freedom inside communism, knowing that any influx of freedom spells the approaching end of the long agony of the Cuban people.

May it be.

Published March 25, 2016, in *The Savvy Street*.

Chapter 3

One Percent Sanders: Do the Math

Here is a 2016 Presidential campaign math problem for you: Subtract one percent from Bernie Sanders, and what remains? That's correct. Nothing.

The senator from Vermont has one issue. The richest Americans are getting richer while the American middle class is getting hosed—and steadily melting away. The solution is to tax the rich to aid the middle class.

And that, essentially, is his whole pitch. Sen. Sanders is a rare American politician who labels himself a "socialist"—a spasm of honesty to be commended. In Europe, such frankness is less rare. Four years ago, French President Francois Hollande was elected on the platform of the Socialist Party. The French economy, now, is frighteningly stagnant and Hollande is grappling with his own colleagues to pass a few measures to increase economic freedom ("Financial Sense" site, March 17, 2016.) Sen. Sanders's socialism, for which he merits an award for heroic cryogenic preservation of a dead idea, has a modern spin. He focuses on the richest "one percent" of Americans—not "the rich" or capitalists—and identifies his victims as the middle class—not "the poor" or the proletariat. This is just politics. If you identify a group for persecution, you may lose their votes, so you'd better keep that group small. Like one percent.

As for the middle class, that is where the votes are. What for the old-time socialists was the exploiting class—the bourgeois, the propertied class, the capitalists—is now, for Sen. Sanders, the victim. In America, today, there are too few "poor"—lower-income, we call them—to elect you President. And anyway, many of them tend not to vote.

The Pitch

"Over 99 percent of all new income generated in the economy has gone to the top 1 percent."

There is the *pitch*. It is not a fast ball or a curve ball. Sen. Sanders has only *one* pitch. In recent years, the top one percent of Americans has gotten *all* the new wealth; the middle class has gotten nothing—or lost.

"In fact, the latest information that we have is that in recent years over 99 percent of all new income generated in the economy has gone to the top 1 percent."

This claim (See *Politifact*, April 19, 2015) rests on the research a couple of economists widely quoted in the press. Those who fact-check such assertions of politicians declare that what Sen. Sanders claims is literally true—and virtually meaningless because it applies in only one limited, idiosyncratic context.

In the years between 2009 and 2013, the average income for the richest one percent of Americans increased from $871,100 annually to $968,000 annually. During the same period, for the other 99 percent of Americans, average income dropped from $44,000 to $43,900.

Here, in one paragraph, is the foundation of the revenant socialism of Sen. Sanders, the math behind the slogan—everything that Bernie Sanders is as a candidate.

If all new wealth is going to one percent of Americans, and all the rest are slipping behind, we have a problem.

This carefully photoshopped statistical picture can be viewed in different lights. Perhaps least important are the data themselves. Nevertheless, that is where we will start.

The Numbers

The income figures used in the comparison are gross income before any taxes and do not include any government benefits. The figures exclude income from Social Security, unemployment compensation, veteran's benefits, Medicare, welfare, tax credits, and food stamps. For tens of millions of Americans within the 99 percent; these benefits are a huge contribution to annual income.

As for the one percent, the income figure is before any taxes that they pay. The Congressional Budget Office reported (The Tax Foundation, January 7, 2014) that in 2014 the top one percent received 15 percent of before-tax income and paid more than 34 percent of all individual income taxes. They paid one-quarter of *all* federal taxes of any kind. At the same time, the bottom 90 percent of taxpayers paid about 32 percent of taxes—less than the top one percent paid.

Bernie, Bernie, did you just not know? Do you just keep forgetting to mention it? Just never had the opportunity to bring it up even once out of the hundreds of times you have waved the one percent-99 percent schtick?

I mentioned that I viewed supplying the statistical context of Sen. Sanders's socialist slogan as the least important aspect of the analysis. I do. Because how much the rich pay in taxes, and how much of that money ends up paying benefits for the middle class, is *not* the justification for "permitting" the existence of great differences in wealth. As one economist pointed out: Your justification for keeping both kidneys— instead of having one taken by government to help a patient who needs it—because, after all, you can be perfectly healthy with one kidney—is that you have an inalienable right to your life, which means your person, your freedom of thought and action, and the work of your mind and hands. The justification is not that you may need the other kidney later or that enough volunteers supply kidneys.

The Principle

The "justification" or principled argument for disparities in wealth is that those who own that wealth earned it by work, trade, and investment of their earnings in a system that permits no one to gain wealth by force and where everyone's right to freedom of action and property is protected equally. The outcomes in such an economic system are justified by one principle: If each person has a right to freedom of thought, freedom of action, and freedom of association—including employment and trade— then *outcomes* of that freedom, including property, are as inalienable as the right to life. One clear implication of the right to property that you have earned is your right to leave it to your heirs, whose right to the property is a derivative of yours.

To give Sen. Sanders his due, he argues that our economic system, today, is skewed to favor the rich—the one percent—and that the system is skewed against the middle class. This is a big issue, which I discuss at length in my book, *Not Half Free: The Myth That America is Capitalist*.)

And I do agree that the "system" is skewed to benefit the wealthy, but especially and overwhelmingly the financial industry, which has become the largest in America as measured by the market capitalization of publicly owned firms.

It is the power of government, today, to intervene in every sphere of the economy—but *particularly* in the money supply, credit, banking, the bond market, and the real-estate mortgage market—which created the conditions and fueled the growth of the financial bubble that burst in 20072008 into the first full financial panic since 1907. *All the solutions proposed by Sen. Sanders would increase the reach and power of government.* The remedy for "crony capitalism," which Sen. Sanders has mentioned—and which is a major theme of my book—is to take away government's power over the operation of the financial industry. That power only corrupts, creates cronies, and, of course, ensures huge contributions to political campaigns.

More "1 Percent" Context

But return for a moment to "the statistic that saved socialism." Notice that the exact period covered by the income comparison is the years after the financial crash, the stock market crash, and the onset of the "Great Recession." A peculiar period to choose for an income comparison, but for Sanders an essential one.

In the financial crash of 2007-2008, the one percent lost trillions of dollars because their wealth is in financial instruments. They lost far more in percentage terms than the rest of the population. By the way, however, even before that the one percent had been losing wealth relative to the general population since 2001, their "best year." That loss just accelerated hugely during the crash.

As the financial markets rallied after 2009, the one percent regained some of those lost trillions. At the same time, much of the population gained little as the "Great Recession" ground on with low employment. Yes, it was a period in which the one percent recovered some lost ground, while the rest of us tended to stagnate.

But I do not think we should alter the direction of the American economy toward greater socialism based on that one period. Do you?

The Ascending Middle Class

I do not want to leave you mourning for the middle class, which, according to Sen. Sanders, is diminishing as we speak. But again, yes, the interventionist-welfare state that has grown up year after year, decade after decade, does tend to favor those who are already wealthy. Why? Because the more power government aggrandizes to itself to intervene to help or hurt business, the more important becomes lobbying, campaign contributions, to ensure that my business, my industry, benefits. *Every proposal by Sen. Sanders would increase the ability of government to determine the fate of businesses—to dispense favors or harm.*

Again, to be fair to Sen. Sanders, he personally appears to refuse to accept such "bribes-in-advance" campaign contributions. Hillary Clinton is alleged to be the champion at getting such support on Wall Street.

But about that vanishing middle class? The *New York Times*, not a bastion of apologetics for capitalism, ran an article in January 2015, with the title, "The Shrinking American Middle Class."

Oh-oh, here comes a serious boost for Sanders socialism.

Not really. The conclusion was that the middle class has been shrinking since at least the mid-Sixties because more Americans have moved into the upper middle class, the affluent class. Note that Sen. Sanders usually refers to "the past 40 years" of the demise of the middle class. The *Times's* statistical charts are from 1967 to 2013, a 46-year period. And during that period, the American middle class shrank. It shrank from 56 percent of the U.S. population to 43 percent—a 13 percent drop. During the same period, the "upper income" cohort, or upper class, grew from 7 percent to 22 percent of the U.S. population—a 15 percent increase.

Holy shit, Bernie. Look at this. All those folks lost from the middle class entered the upper income class. During the same period, the percentage of Americans in the lower-income class declined from 40 percent of Americans to 34 percent.

Hey, I'm not making this up, Bernie. Check the *Times.*

Tell me you just forgot, Bernie. Tell me you forgot to mention that the vanishing middle class was rising into the upper class? And both the lower-income and middle-income groups were shrinking.

Now, where is the truth, if any, in what Sen. Sanders says? Well, he does not say it, exactly, but maybe he could use this on the campaign trail. We have discussed the 46-year period, 1967-2013. But during the 21st Century, there has been a 10-year slowdown—the first in our recorded history—of wage growth, and especially in families that qualify as high income. Since the year 2000, the income of the American middle class *has* shrunk; for the first time, fewer moved up into the upper class.

For the most recent eight years, of course, we have had the most "progressive" President in our history, Barack Obama. We have had the financial panic and "Great Recession" left us by President George W. Bush, which I discussed above. But those are not the reasons suggested by the *Times* for this first-ever slowdown, for what the *Times* calls "the great 21st Century slowdown in wages growth."

The *Times* suggests other reasons. There are far more Hispanic families, including millions of legal and illegal immigrants. About half of black and almost half of Hispanic households are lower income. The incidence of single mothers, unwed mothers, has increased, and that is a sure formula for poverty; married couples where both partners work tend to move into the upper class. Americans under 30 years old, especially families under 30, are way overrepresented among the "wage slowdown" victims. They are a very vocal constituency for Sen. Sanders.

In sum, for the 40 years that Sen. Sanders likes to mention, the middle class has shrunk *by joining the upper class*. For the past decade, largely during the Obama administration, the middle class has suffered shrinking income for the first time since measurements began. The reasons cited by the *Times*—the influx of Hispanic immigrants, the change of family composition from two adults to one, the under-30 Americans who are not getting an economic grip—seem to have little to do with the allegedly malign influence of the one percent who have recovered wealth lost in the financial crash.

The socialist proposals of Sen. Sanders to remedy this non-problem would increase the size, power, and reach of government in the American economy. And yet, it was this government intervention that enabled the great financial crash of 2007-2008 and the Great Recession that followed. It is the root cause of the distortions of the U.S economy that do, in fact, promote "crony capitalism."

The only idea or slogan that defines the candidacy of Sen. Bernard Sanders is true in an excruciatingly delimited context, but in any broader context, it is meaningless. The real causes of the recent decade-long decline in middle class incomes have little to do with the wealth of the one percent.

The root premises of socialism are inconsistent with the right to life, freedom of thought and action, free trade and exchange, and the wealth that may result.

The International 1 Percent

Americans who have narrowed their context to their own country, their own era, and their own present economic circumstances should think carefully before endorsing the socialist principle of Sen. Sanders, which implies the sacrifice of the wealthy to the needs of others. If this principle is asserted as a serious moral claim, it must rest upon relationships among all human beings, not just Americans.

The international agency, Oxfam, created to combat famine in the world, has turned recently (there seem to be no more famines to fight) to advocating worldwide wealth "redistribution." Except that it really is not "redistribution" because wealth was never initially "distributed." It was created by the ideas and efforts of individuals.

Oxfam has pointed out, with media fanfare, that one percent of the world's population soon will possess half of the world's total wealth. For Oxfam, the implications, consistent with the principle of socialism, are the same as those drawn by Sen. Sanders. Seize and "redistribute" wealth.

If you are an American, you most probably are on the Global Rich List, a website devoted to disparities in worldwide income. If your annual income is $32,400 a year, then you are in the top one percent of the global rich. Bernie Sanders is talking about *you* and your ill-gotten gains.

As I have written elsewhere, there is great worldwide economic unfairness, but it has nothing to do with the ideas of Sen. Sanders. The remedies of the economic unfairness that put the undeserving in the top one percent of global income are in exact contradiction to the socialism of Sen. Sanders.

What is "unfairly" distributed around the world? Economic freedom. The national income levels of nations correlate consistently with their degree of economic freedom. The countries with the greatest degree of laissez-faire capitalism—or, today, the most remnants of that system— are the wealthiest. They have liberated the minds, actions, innovation, and drive that create great wealth. They have made possible Bill Gates of Microsoft; Warren Buffett of Berkshire Hathaway; Larry Ellison of Oracle; the Waltons of Wal-Mart; Jeff Bezos of Amazon; Larry Page of Google—who are all among the top 20 American billionaires on the *Forbes* list.

If their names are familiar, it is because they have achieved their fortunes with products that transformed the life of the American consumer, and have ushered America and the globe into the future. All started their lives in middle-class families, and some not even that— Larry Ellison came from a single-mother home in Brooklyn, and was then put up for adoption. Most of the innovations that define the American present were originated in America by middle-class men and women who rose during their lifetimes to the one percent.

Sen. Sanders is not wrong that the America economy has fallen on bitter times. He is not wrong that too much of Wall Street garners its extravagant profits thanks to government. Today, Wall Street begs the Federal Reserve daily to continue its inflationary policies—because the new money conjured up by the Fed arrives first in banks and on Wall Street. Sen. Sanders would respond to this grotesque abuse of government intervention in the American economy by increasing it.

Socialism substitutes government power and the decision-making of politicians and bureaucrats for the complex interaction of individuals daily in free trade, free exchange, free choice—manifestations of the free mind in producing wealth.

Economic freedom, the limited government, *always and everywhere* results in the wealth of nations.

Published March 28, 2016, in *The Savvy Street*.

Chapter 4

Clinton Versus Trump on Climate Change

I recently published a personal manifesto on the controversial question—a.k.a. adult pillow fight—of global warming/climate change. The weather used to be a safe topic of conversation, avoiding politics and religion, but now epitomizes the type of divisive political question that scuttles family reunions. Critics of "Big Climate Alarmism," and I am one, compare it point for point with religious dogma. In reply, advocates of the view that CO_2 generated by man's activities is heating up the Earth's atmosphere, with potentially calamitous consequences, assert that anyone who fails to see the Big Truth is like those wackos who deny that the WWII Nazi-extermination-camp Holocaust ever occurred. Who would have thought that discussing the weather conditions of not tomorrow but in 2050 could end lifelong friendships?

Here, I am not going to debate global warming/climate change (but see "Why I Deny Big Climate Alarmism," *Savvy Street*, September 18, 2016). I have another agenda.

In the 2016 U.S. presidential campaign, which at present demands our breathless attention to personal health issues, Clinton's email servers, Trump's alleged admiration of Russian dictator Vladimir Putin, Trump's "birther" obsession, and Clinton's supposed deceptions, there nevertheless are remarkably bold differences between the candidates that bear upon the future the Great Republic and the world.

A Stark Policy Difference

One example is the difference between the candidates' positions on global warming/climate change. True, through the angry noise of the campaign, amplified in the echo chambers of the media, I barely discern any substantive issue. And yet, five minutes of Googling reveals a wellarticulated, black-and-white difference between the candidates.

Here is the League of Conservation Voters with admirable neutrality presenting the candidates in their own words on climate change, updated through August 2016. Trump in an interview with the *Miami Herald* on August 11 of this year:

"I'm not a big believer in manmade climate change. There could be some impact, but I don't believe it's a devastating impact. I would say that it goes up, it goes down, and I think it's very much like this over the years. We'll see what happens…

"But certainly, climate has changed. You know, they used to call it global warming. They've had many different names…they call it extreme weather. They always change the name to encapsulate everything.

"The problem we have is our businesses are suffering. Our businesses are unable to compete in this country because other countries aren't being forced to do what our businesses are being forced to do and it makes us noncompetitive, which is something that I feel very strongly about. And I feel that it puts us at a great economic disadvantage for jobs…"

This is an amazingly succinct summary of the "climate change" issue and its implications, especially considering this is just an answer to one interview question along the campaign trail.

All right, and here is Clinton's campaign Web site quoting her own words:

"Climate change is an urgent threat and a defining challenge of our time. It threatens our economy, our national security, and our children's health and futures…

"Hillary's plan will deliver on the pledge President Obama made at the Paris climate conference—without relying on climate deniers in Congress to pass new legislation. She will reduce greenhouse gas emissions by up to 30 percent in 2025 relative to 2005 levels and put the country on a path to cut emissions more than 80 percent by 2050."

I said something nice about Trump's remarks so, to maintain balance, I should say something nice about Clinton's, right? Damned if I can think of anything. The hypothesis of a dangerous global warming trend has been called "a busted flush." Yes, there was a warming trend, a total of about 0.7 of one degree Celsius, from 1888 to 1998. This is remarkably brief in climate history. Think of the coming and going of ice ages and interglacial periods every 10,000 years or so for millions of years. The 118-year trend meant little unless you could point to some new, decisive factor entering the picture. The New Left, around 1970, cried with one voice: Yes, capitalism! We knew it! Okay, we were wrong that capitalism causes wars, and wrong that it impoverishes the masses, but, yes! It is screwing up the climate, dooming us all. It was the philosopher Ayn Rand who first, with incredible prescience, and luminous insight, identified this as the Left's next attempt to destroy capitalism (see *The New Left: The Anti-Industrial Revolution*).

But in 1998, the hottest year since 1888, global warming went on vacation. Depending upon who is measuring it, that vacation lasted 16 years (agreed by both sides) or is still going (dissenters). This busted the flush. Some one hundred computer models ("General Climate Models"), created at a cost of hundreds of millions of dollars to taxpayers to predict the extent of global warming 50 to 100 years from now, failed to predict what happened in any year after 1998. For the long years of no global warming, the theory was used by politicians to enact regulations costing hundreds of billions of dollars, raising the costs of energy for everyone, and to subsidize pre-Industrial Revolution sources of energy: wind and the sun.

Okay, here is <u>Trump</u>, again, speaking to the North Dakota Petroleum Council on May 26, 2016:

"President Obama entered the United States into the Paris Climate Accords unilaterally, and without the permission of Congress. This agreement gives foreign bureaucrats control over how much energy we use right here in America. These actions have denied millions of

Americans access to the energy wealth sitting under our feet."

He is referring to the new methods of drilling for oil and new innovations in capturing natural gas that woke the world suddenly by thrusting the United States into first place among oil producers, promising for the first time independence from Middle Eastern oil that has transferred literally generations of wealth from United States, Western Europe, and Japan to Middle Eastern nations such as Saudi Arabia and Qatar that use their wealth to subsidize the worldwide promulgation of radical Islam, including ISIS. Almost immediately, U.S. President Barrack Obama and his then Secretary of State, Hillary Clinton, attacked this new industry with regulations and special taxes. They pledged at the Paris Conference in 2015 to shut down the fossil fuel industry in favor of wind and solar power. I can't help saying, "Wow, congratulations, Saudi Arabia and Venezuela. You have great partners in the United States." And to give Clinton the last word from the *Washington Post*, April 14, 2016, quoting her at a Brooklyn campaign debate:

"Let's talk about the global environmental crisis. Starting in 2009 as your Secretary of State, I worked with President Obama to bring China and India to the table for the very first time, to get a commitment out of them that they would begin to address their own greenhouse gas emissions.

"I continued to work on that throughout the four years as Secretary of State, and I was very proud that President Obama and America led the way to the agreement that was finally reached in Paris with 195 nations committing to take steps to actually make a difference in climate change."

A Choice Not an Echo

Now, here we enjoy what once was called "a choice, not an echo."

How serious a choice? If that means getting into the debate over climate change/global warming, I'm not going there. I refer you to my statement referenced above, reached after extensive research, thought, and debate. You can read daily in the mainstream press reports of the devastation supposedly attributable to man-made temperature change. For the dissent, I recommend *Climate Change: The Facts*, published in a revised edition in 2015. Developed by Institute of Public Affairs in Melbourne, Australia, it brings together in one statement the world's leading scientists, economists, journalists, public policy analysts, and politicians on the "*I deny*" side of the debate.

What I would state, here, given the clear policy differences expounded by the two candidates, is what is at stake.

One of the world's leading proponents of the global warming theory and its urgent importance is William McKibben. In the August 15 issue of *The New Republic*, in an article emblazed across many pages, he argued that the threat of global warming/climate change has reached crisis proportions comparable to the militant rise of national socialist (Naz.) Germany in the late 1930's. The article begins with the breathless reportorial description of an invasion of the United States and other parts of the world. Territory has been lost, the death toll is soaring, and key targets have been bombed out. The invader is global warming and t is winning.

The recuired response is a governmental command economy that mobilizes the American economy on a scale, and with an urgency and scope, greater even than the heroic mobilization of U.S. industry to meet the challenge of WWII. Read it. Within a few years, virtually all of America's fundamental energy industry must be mothballed; every economic resource and means directed, by government dictate, to building hundreds of huge solar energy and wind energy complexes. This is a call for the command economy of economic dictatorship beyond anything America has imagined let alone experienced. Arguably in a reputable journal of policy opinion in America.

Well, McKibben can ring the tocsin from parish to parish across America, but does it cost us anything?

It does. The impact of what Clinton versus Trump proposes will translate in real life, real time, into laws enacted and regulations, rules, and requirements promulgated to implement those laws. The U.S. Chamber of Commerce reported that "During the eight years of the Obama administration alone, regulators have laid down 600 major rules (rules that the agencies *themselves* estimate will cost more than $100 million each, per year, for compliance). That breaks down to 81 major rules per year or approximately one new $100-million rule every three days the government is open."

What area of federal government's dictation to U.S. businesses requires this barrage of rules? Quite naturally, it is the area that Clinton characterizes as putting the future of life on Earth and of our children at risk. Focusing in a bit more closely, there also are *billion-dollar-plus* compliance rules. Between 2000 and 2015, the Environmental Protection Agency promulgated 20 such rules at a compliance cost of $101 billion dollars. *All other federal agencies* combined, during the same period, promulgated 14 major rules at a compliance cost of $22.9 billion.

Well, today, our government is reckoned in trillions of dollars. What is the harm? The Chamber of Commerce report offers examples. Here is one.

"Meanwhile, the Clean Power Plan, or CPP, upends the entire U.S. energy sector by requiring states to drastically cut emissions from traditional power plants. CPP would increase average electricity prices in 40 states, costing households up to $79 billion. In a sense, EPA's new power plant rule forces an industry to do something that's technologically impossible. Thankfully, the Supreme Court stayed, or blocked, the rule from implementation until pending lawsuits play out in the judicial system."

Yes, something is at stake when the chattering classes, including our candidates for president in 2016, have a difference of opinion over "Big Climate Alarmism."

What characterizes Hillary Clinton is pride in what the Obama administration has accomplished in the McKibben "war of the worlds" scenario. Her position is that more must done, building on these policies, and must be done urgently.

Donald Trump is a "global warming denier." To me, that begins to sound like an honorable designation. He seems to understand in an easy, commonsensical way that the climate changes; he understands that theories of climate change evolve; and he understands that one live scenario—advanced by solar scientists, now in disrepute for contradicting Big Climate alarmism—is that we face a coming ice age. And that to devote all resources to mothballing fossil fuel energy, and to erecting a worldwide structure of wind and solar power, would leave humanity utterly naked and unprepared for a new ice age. Leave humanity victims of the fatally wrong decision for humankind, promoted by the scientists it had come to trust, who only wanted to be accepted by their peers and make a good living.

But Trump does not buy either scenario. He says, as quoted, "Let's see." But, for now, he says, do not make the American economy and jobs hostage to weather forecasting 50 or 100 years into the future. I urge you to check out my links to both Trump statements and the Clinton statements. You wouldn't know from the media, even this late in the campaign, that both have made substantive statements on this issue dozens of times even in the last month.

Whoever becomes the next President will exercise direct control in this area. Recent decades have seen a shift of law-making out of Congress and into the Executive. Yes, "laws" are enacted by Congress—let's say, 150 a year—but drafting and promulgating regulations, rules, and requirements to implement those laws has been handed over to bureaucrats in the departments and agencies of the Executive. They promulgate, say, 3,000 new regulations a year, including dozens each year, each with \$100-million compliance costs for the economy. The more regulations, the larger their domain, the greater their power.

The next president will appoint the leadership of every department and agencies, give them marching orders, and oversee their compliance with her or his vision. Trump could choose appointees and give directives to bridle the EPA and the other agencies that energetically dictate to America the demands of Big Climate alarmists. At a minimum, and immediately, he could purge the nation's top bureaucracy of those who carry water for organizations like Greenpeace.

You will make up your own mind, of course; that is your responsibility and privilege as a voter in America. My point is that what you decide will make a big difference. This is an important election. Who would have thought?

Published September 23, 2016 in *The Savvy Street*.

Chapter 5

Democrats Versus "White Nationalists"?

Paul Krugman says he can tell you why, shamefully and against all odds, Donald Trump is running about neck and neck with Hillary Clinton one month before election day. It is simple: Donald Trump is a "white nationalist"—one who believes that the national identity of America is racially white—and so, too, are enough Americans to make the election unforgivably (in Krugman's view) close.

"Part of the answer is that a lot more Americans than we'd like to imagine are white nationalists at heart. Indeed, implicit appeals to racial hostility have long been at the core of Republican strategy; Mr. Trump became the G.O.P. nominee by saying outright what his opponents tried to convey with dog whistles."

Note on jargon: "Dog whistle" is a metaphor for political language that communicates a message to the intended audience—the "dogs"— while being inaudible, because subsonic, to human beings. (By golly, I think I hear a dog whistle *right now*, in Krugman's subsonic message that many of those voting for Trump are not truly human.) Thus, Krugman has long argued that Ronald Reagan dog-whistled his way to a whitesupremacist victory by using such terms as "welfare queen" to characterize women who live on welfare and an array of other government payments.

Krugman is the white knight, the idealized champion, moving America as rapidly as possible toward socialism. A Nobel laureate in economics, Ivy League professor, and columnist for the *New York Times*, Krugman proclaimed his socialism in his book, *Conscience of A Liberal*, a deliberate parallel with *Conscience of a Conservative* by Barry Goldwater. Krugman explains that "liberal" in America equates with "social democrat" in Europe. I will argue that the more precise term is

"fascist"—one who aspires to elect a government that is the fascist (national socialist) versus communistic variant of socialism.

If Krugman puts white nationalism *first* among motives for supporting Trump, he accuses what is called the "American heartland" of bigotry. Much of the South, Midwest, Northwest, parts of New England, and some Mid-Atlantic states now are for Trump. Almost half of America, on Krugman's map, is heavily white nationalist, yearning for a racially pure United States that, in fact, never existed, that they never experienced, but that Paul Krugman divines in their hearts.

Krugman is plugging this view on behalf of Clinton's because she cannot accuse half of the electorate of being racists; but if, as she says, Trump is *obviously* a racist, xenophobe, misogynist, and homophobe, then what is she saying about his supporters? Answer: Only a bigot could vote for Trump.

Clinton's Problem: An "Adversarial" Press?

Mr. Krugman does say that "racially motivated voters" are still a minority—and therefore Clinton is still leading–but now, he says, she has run into "a buzz saw of adversarial reporting from the mainstream press…" That statement takes us into an alternate reality I do not recognize. Krugman offers a couple examples such as criticism of the Clinton Foundation and the 30,000 missing emails. But I would have said that never in my adult life, in any election, have I seen even remotely the remorseless attack in 2016 on one candidate—Donald Trump.

Krugman virtually assumes that in terms of the *issues* there are no remotely plausible grounds for favoring Trump. My personal testimony is the opposite: Despite some of Trump's behavior, rough comments, and stage antics, I am drawn to his believable positions on some crucial issues. My reaction to debate #1? Relief. That maybe I can live with the Trump of debate #1 for the sake of his policies.

We are talking about the first debate, so I will give an example of what I mean:

The first question to the candidates: What would you do to create jobs?

Clinton replied: "I want to invest in you…" and with no explanatory transition…"jobs in infrastructure, advanced manufacturing, innovation and technology, clean energy…" [Are those federal government jobs? What "investment" will create them?] "…make the economy fairer, "raise the national minimum wage," "equal pay for women's work," "profit sharing," "paid family leave," "debt free college," "make the wealthy pay their share," "close corporate tax loopholes." [Obama didn't manage to do any of that in eight years?]

Trump replied: "[S]top companies from leaving the United States…" [Companies have the jobs.] How to stop them? Slash the corporate tax rate from 35 percent to 15 percent. And, if they leave, don't exempt them from import taxes when they send their goods back to the United States to sell in competition with other foreign suppliers.

Clinton opens a menu of voting hot buttons. Trump advances a proposal to turn around the flight abroad of U.S. corporations. Giving businesses a huge break (remember, everyone who works for a business also pays personal income tax) is SO painfully politically incorrect that it might work. Businesses create real jobs; businesses will hire as many workers as can, on net, contribute to their profits; profits are hugely affected by taxes. The two chief aspects of competition with foreign countries for businesses are 1. wages, and 2. taxes. Can we slash wages? Government does not control wages, at least not yet, except for states setting a minimum wage, which causes unemployment because businesses lose money when required to pay workers more than they contribute to profit. The big losers are minority teenagers, who need entry level jobs at market wages to get onto the career ladder. But we can cut corporate taxes, creating a far more attractive environment for business.

Trump's proposal: simple, direct, powerful. Clinton's: a memorized list of promises to everyone. (Given this tendency to rote citation in one answer of a dozen or more voter hot-button promises, some called her

"over-prepared" for the debates.) She was not "over prepared," she was "too obviously programmed."

On the first question of the evening, the distance between Trump and Clinton became clear.

Here are some issues that impel those who are not white nationalists to hope in coming weeks Trump continues to present a stature we associate with the White House. It is obvious to me that the lifelong politician, Washington insider, 100 percent left-liberal establishment candidate, Clinton, has no business as chief executive or commander-inchief.

■   Addressing the New York Economic Club, Trump pledged to halt all new regulations until a thorough review can be made of their costs and benefits. There is wide agreement today that federal regulations are a $2.0 trillion annual drag on the U.S. economy. The Obama administration, so far, has added $100 billion to that annual load. All of Clinton's hundreds of promises imply nothing but acceleration of federal regulation.

■   Trump will not implement the political agenda of "environmentalism," which is based upon the controversial hypothesis of "catastrophic global warming" over the next century. Clinton, by contrast, calls catastrophic global warming America's greatest future threat. The goal of the radical ideological environmentalists is to shut down America's fossil-fuel producers (natural gas, oil, and coal), the utilities and other companies that rely on them, and the automobile and other transportation systems based on them—in short. the energy that powers our economy. To replace them? Government dictates to direct every economic resource into construction of gigantic systems of solar and wind energy—now the most expensive in the world. This is not the *future*; the Obama administration that Clinton emulates and hopes to continue promulgated *more* billion-dollar-a-year-plus regulations on environment and energy than in all other areas combined.

■   Trump pays little attention to the "identity politics" that obsesses Hillary Clinton, who plays to the special demands of women versus men, Blacks versus Whites, illegal immigrants versus citizens, the

"rich" versus the middle class, Black Americans versus the police, gayslesbians-transsexuals versus the population at large—every imaginable variant on the theme that society is a ceaseless struggle of the "oppressed" for "social justice" at the hands of their "oppressors." As President, she would choose enough new Supreme Court justices to create a majority faction of pure advocates for the claims of these supposedly aggrieved groups, replacing the slim Court majority that has tended to view all Americans as having the same equal rights to legal protection, opportunity, striving, and success—but no special privileges. Mr. Trump, we know, would not overturn the long-standing "the Reagan majority" in making his appointments.

■   Well, what about the charge that tens of millions of white Americans support Trump, and not the accelerating "democratic socialism" of Clinton, because they want a racially pure white America? Trump's vow to deal decisively with crime in predominantly black neighborhoods, and in cities at large, is viewed by Krugman as "dog whistle" racial politics.

Dealing with Black Crime—Dog Whistle Politics?

Urban policy analyst, Heather MacDonald, of New York's leading think-tank, the Manhattan Institute, reviewed Department of Justice statistics on race and violent crimes (except murder, a tiny percentage). Some of the highlights:

"First, we find that during the 2012/2013 period, blacks committed an average of 560,600 violent crimes against whites, whereas whites committed only 99,403 such crimes against blacks. This means blacks were the attackers in 84.9 percent of the violent crimes involving blacks and whites."

"Interestingly, we find that violent interracial crime involving blacks and Hispanics occurs in almost the same proportions as black/white crime: Blacks are the attacker's 82.5 percent of the time, while Hispanics are attackers only 17.5 percent of the time."

"Using figures for the 2013 racial mix of the population–62.2 percent white, 17.1 percent Hispanic, 13.2 percent black–we can calculate the average likelihood of a person of each race attacking the other. A black is 27 times more likely to attack a white and 8 times more likely to attack a Hispanic than the other way around."

Mr. Trump insists that America has a "huge crime problem" in its black neighborhoods and cities at large and that the answer—surprise! – is law enforcement. Mr. Krugman says Trump is appealing to bigotry of white nationalists. Hillary Clinton is a cheerleader for the group "Black Lives Matter," which blames the entire problem on, well, white nationalists in the law-enforcement system.

Hillary Clinton's "Tribalism"

Permit me an aside: Voices across America in this election are trying to persuade white Americans to view themselves as a *tribe*. Most Americans don't do this, viewing themselves as individuals as likely to disagree as to agree with another white person—you know, the way I am disagreeing with Hillary Clinton and Paul Krugman. But the new and truly dangerous Liberal-Left ("democratic socialist") chorus today is that "whites" are a tribe—with collective interests, collective responsibility, collective guilt. This tribe owes the black tribe "social justice," especially income equality, and perhaps historical reparations.

I first encountered this insight in an article in *The Federalist* by David Marcus. In "How Anti-White Rhetoric Is Fueling White Nationalism," he points at the potential catastrophe that Clinton is risking fueling a campaign that has won her 90 percent or more of the Black vote. Of course, she directed the same race-tinged rhetoric against Bernard Sanders that she used against Barrack Obama in the 2008 Democratic primary. This is not a charge leveled by her enemies. In its editorial endorsing Clinton in 2008, the *New York Times* warned: **"Mrs. Clinton will be making a terrible mistake — for herself, her party and for the nation — if she continues to press her candidacy through negative campaigning with disturbing racial undertones…"** Eight years later, she is still doing it, this time to Trump—and the *Times* endorsed her-again.

The entire article by David Marcus is "must" reading. He writes: "White people are being asked—or pushed—to take stock of their whiteness and identify with it more. This is a remarkably bad idea. The last thing our society needs is for white people to feel more tribal. The result of this tribalism will not be a catharsis of white identity, improving equality for non-whites. It will be resentment towards being the only tribe not given the special treatment bestowed by victimhood"—by being
"oppressed."

Beneath the tattered, flimsy guise of combating racism, Clinton is hyping racial suspicions and racial tensions for all they're worth to sweep the black vote. For all her polished rhetoric and grand-motherly folksiness, she is leading too many black Americans—there are certainly individual exceptions—back into a darker time in America and history.

I will not vote for Hillary Clinton. She represents no more than an acceleration of our nation's slide toward outright socialism. If she wins, be prepared for a surge toward socialism not of public ownership type, but an increasing economic dictation that better fits the definition of economic fascism. And the constant resentment, anger, and street riots stirred up by identity politics--from the media to schools to colleges—fits surprisingly well with another aspect of fascism: seething racial, economic, and other collective resentments exploited by power-seeking politicians. Then, by 2020, perhaps we will be ready for a Green Party president, like Jill Stein, who is openly against the Industrial Revolution that ushered in modernity's unprecedented prosperity in the developed world—and is the hope of millions in India, China, and elsewhere to escape poverty.

Still Watching, Still Worrying

There are issues, of course, where I strongly disagree with Trump. When he entered the Republican primaries, he began to pay lip service to the "right to life." No one can win the Republican nomination without doing so, but when he won, he named perhaps the best-known "right to life" advocate in Congress, Michael Pence, as his vice-presidential candidate. My guess is that a President Trump will downplay the issue— as has every Republican president. But if Pence succeeds him to office, we have a problem. Second, I would like to know more (wouldn't we all) about Trump's proposed strategy toward Iran and the nuclear deal; a foreign policy imperative of the next administration is to honestly scrutinize Iran actions, immediately publicize and protest violations, and, if Iran persists, start escalating sanctions. If the deal can be saved by enforcement, instead of scrapped, it will be by Trump, not Clinton.

What most troubles me is Trump's personality. I don't mean the endless petty posing of the press as more politically correct than the boorish Trump, but the bully we see, the insecure ego that brooks no disagreement, that must giggle and quip and boast in response to criticism. Often, he is justified. His response to Khizer Khan's silly attack at the Democratic National Convention was to be expected—and was right. But for heaven's sake, keep it dignified—presidential.

I am encouraged that a lifelong businessman could be in the White House, for the first time *ever*—but troubled by Trump's apparently glamor- and power-seeking drive to build a real-estate empire with overleveraged businesses and its spectacular debt collapse in the mid-1990s. After this over-extension, fully 20 years ago, Trump faced bankruptcy court, but has recouped his losses and apparently risen to new heights of wealth. He described the disaster and redemption in *The Art of the Comeback*. America right now could use a comeback.

This essay concludes with no call to arms. I cannot charge forward under the Trump colors. The final two Presidential debates probably will make up my mind.

For readers attracted to the Libertarian Party candidate, Gary Johnson, I offer solace. If you vote for Johnson, you are not necessarily "throwing away" your vote. Of course, you are making a statement about principle and the libertarian vote in this election might be five times the size of that in the last election. But, if it troubles you that, in practice, you are advancing the candidacy of Clinton, there is good news. Most likely, your vote for Johnson hurts Clinton and favors Trump in pivotal states such as Colorado.

Have it both ways. Krugman and I, by different logics, are certain that you will pay heavily for a mistake in November.

Published October 7, 2016, in *The Savvy Street.*

Chapter 6

Isn't $1.9 Trillion A Year Lost to Regulation Enough?

If Hillary Clinton and Donald Trump ever finish sparring over personal health, illicit emails, and Vladimir Putin's qualities as a leader, we can hope they will address the fundamental choice that faces the American electorate in 2016: How much of our lives will be controlled by government? How much will be left to the choices of Americans individually and through their private businesses, institutions, and organizations?

The question goes to the heart of government power versus individual liberty. It is the question that defined America. And today it has application to every single action of government, and, unfortunately, directly or indirectly, every decision in every American life. Any candidate who fails to address that question seriously, credibly, and often may be assumed to be taking for granted that politics, and the office they seek, is exclusively about the exercise of power, how to increase it— and probably how much they crave such power.

How urgent is this issue? Consider just one yardstick of government power over our jobs, incomes, businesses, health, consumer choices, and, well—to repeat—everything else. That yardstick is federal government regulation.

The Cost of Regulations

At the end of May this year, as the primaries heated up and conventions loomed, two economists at the Heritage Institute wrote that the Obama administration has been responsible for an explosion of the

"regulatory state." Since his election in 2009, the Executive Branch has promulgated 229 "major" regulations, regulations each costing more than
$100 million annually (according to the regulatory agencies themselves). The annual cost of just these new major regulations is now $108 billion a year. Restriction of innovations and loss of opportunity resulting from the regulations are not included in the price tag.

The Competitive Enterprise Institute (CEI) focused on just one year of the Obama Administration, 2014, and looked at all, not just "major," regulations. In that year, the Administration finalized some 3,600 new regulations and proposed 2,300 more. Regulations, rules, and restrictions already in place, said the Institute, impose an estimated $1.9 trillion annual "drag" on the America economy. The Office of Management and the Budget reported that government demands for information alone— nothing else—require some nine billion (not million) hours of paperwork each year.

A U.S. Chamber of Commerce report this month explained that regulation-making power has undergone a vast geologic shift away from Congress to the Executive Branch. Each year, Congress may enact 150 laws but bureaucrats then cook up 3,000 rules, including dozens of those "major" rules" costing the economy more than $100 million annually.

Because Mr. Trump has made bringing manufacturing "back to America" a theme of his campaign, look at just the headlines of a recent report by the National Association of Manufacturers. It estimates the average cost to a U.S. company of federal regulation at $9,991 per employee—21 percent of its payroll. But, when it comes to manufacturers in America, the costs of regulations nearly double to $19,564 per employee.

Halt the Growth of Regulations

Staying with this one yardstick of the growth of government power at the expense of individual choice and freedom of enterprise, voters can demand of our Presidential candidate's explicit commitments and credible plans on government regulation. Hillary Clinton is known for detailoriented recommendations on economic questions, but focused on increasing taxes on the wealthy and spending the proceeds on new programs. As recently as September 15, Donald Trump, however, presenting his economic plan to the New York Economic Club, pledged to end all new federal regulation until a review of regulation, its costs and benefits, can be completed. The issue of regulation, it would seem, is once again "in play."

Making no judgment on the credibility of the candidates, it nevertheless is worth commenting that if Mr. Trump is seriously committed to challenging the growth of federal regulation, he would have exceptional power as president. As mentioned, Congress has ceded to the Executive and its agencies virtual plenipotentiary power in formulating and enforcing new regulations. The next President of the United States has the power to appoint department and agency heads, and to issue Executive orders, to curb the growth of new regulations with hundredmillion-dollar price tags.

The prospect is exciting because reigning in regulation goes to the heart of the struggle over government power versus freedom and is where the next President has an extraordinarily free hand. No excuses about cooperation from Congress. No delays.

Although Mr. Trump has floated the idea of zero new regulations pending review, the ideal situation would be if both candidates "took the pledge" that regulation-making would be halted pending a thorough, public, hard-headed review of costs and benefits. And that review would examine, at every step, lost time, lost options, lost opportunities of Americans.

The pledge alone would highlight Washington's eight-year orgy of regulation writing.

Published October 2, 2016, by *The Atlas Society*.

Chapter 7

Policy Differences Buried Under Malicious Attacks

We can conclude, with confidence, that a determined sleaze attack, if taken up by the press with amoral ferocity, can swing an American Presidential election in the direction desired by the media.

A Fox News presidential poll today reported Hillary Clinton's seven-point lead over Donald Trump. This is outside the poll's "margin of error" and the many subcategories of poll results confirm consistent gains for Clinton since the press set off the video bomb a week ago.

The video was leaked from NBC to the *Washington Post*, in case you have been hiking in the Australian outback, and was recorded 11 years ago, without the knowledge of those recorded—an accidental "hot mic"— and held for more than a decade before being released two days before the second Presidential debate. The video, taken on a soap opera set, recorded guest Donald Trump and a network staffer, in a private, rather overexcited, boasting session, with Trump saying that given star status a guy could walk up to certain women and "grab their pussy" without preliminaries.

Not the sort of macho boast, or joke, any guy would choose to have recorded, and, more than a decade later, become perhaps the most replayed and discussed video clip every released on the world. But there was a logic in the timing of the release and for the sudden virtually exclusive focus on this video by the media to the exclusion of all else. (On a recent day, the front page of the *New York Times* presented 17 articles and opinion pieces all attacking the candidacy of Trump with a dozen or so about the "pussy attack."

Only One Issue, Now

In effect, America's so-called "opinion makers" chose to anoint this the ONLY issue now worth considering in the coming Presidential election. Any voter wishing to consider other matters must turn from the mainstream media to other sources. Play pussy or don't play at all.

Well, ask of a folly only what it accomplishes. On a forced diet of repeating the story with comments, analyses, and tirades, the American electorate in about a week turned from supporting the Trump candidacy—which had been neck-and-neck with Clinton—to putting Trump well behind. No sooner had THAT been breathlessly accomplished by the media than it launched that nationwide blitz: Trump candidacy defeated.

Hey, Americans. Don't bother to vote on November 8, the election has been decided. It's Hillary by a landslide.

What else did the folly accomplish? Well, before the October video surprise, Trump's supporters were looking at the issues, at what Mr. Trump stated as his positions and his promises. Trump? Positions? Nah! *What* positions?

The Supreme Court. The next President will make appointments changing the Court for decades. Trump names possible appointees in the tradition of Justice Scalia to uphold the *U.S. Constitution*. In the second debate, Clinton listed more than a dozen race, gender, and age related social goals for the newly configured Court. She did not mention the *U.S. Constitution*. Trump said: Uphold the *U.S. Constitution.*

The Economy. Trump and Clinton both focus on jobs. Trump says cut the corporate income tax from 35 percent to 15 percent, on average, across all businesses. That will give corporations a powerful incentive to stay in the U.S. or repatriate. Hillary lists more than a dozen vague promises such as "equal pay," fairness," "minimum wage," and "make the rich pay"—each with big voter constituencies—without ever showing how they connect with more jobs. They don't.

Health. Trump says repeal the Affordable Care Act ("Obamacare"), encourage competition across state lines by health insurance companies now protected from competition to offer better plans, and create health care savings plans and tax exemptions for medical expenses. The theme is: Move back toward the private sector. Clinton says revise and strengthen Obama Care and…well, the list is simply too long to reproduce—promising to meet dozens of specific demands of various voter blocs.

Energy and the Environment. Trump says accelerate the huge advance in U.S. and Canadian energy production made possible by technology su:h as fracking and natural gas storage. Those advances several years ago made America the #1 energy producer in the world for the first time in decades. In sight, after decades, was U.S. energy independence from the Middle East authoritarian regimes. Mr. Trump says that, sure, "global warming" exists, but there is no evidence that it presents a long-term threat; forecasting the weather half a century or more from now cannot justify elimination of our robust fossil fuel economy, dramatically higher energy prices, and casting aside independence.

Clinton says that "global warming and climate change" are the single greatest crisis facing America. Ms. Clinton wants to dismantle America's energy infrastructure and build a gigantic system of windmills and solar panels at any cost.

Education. Trump says education is a state and local matter, but all new fur.ds from the federal government should be directed toward "schools of choice," charter schools, and other experiments in alternatives to the public education monopoly that is failing its captive students, especially in African-American neighborhoods. Clinton, with almost 100 percent support of National Education Association (NEA) members, who enjoy a legally enforced monopoly through the public schools. and represent one of the largest lobby groups in America, says permit no competition with the public education system. Just pour in more money; that will solve the problem. The NEA loves it.

Immigration. Trump says there are now some 11 million illegal ("undocumented") aliens in the United States. These residents began their stay by violating our law, are illegal and so cannot legally work within our system, and cannot pay taxes, social security payments, and other obligations, but do enjoy many benefits supported by taxpayers. Trump says that in a country founded on law and equal application of the law, this is intolerable. The illegal must go through the process, now on the books, to become legal; new illegals, pouring into the country every day, must be stopped. Clinton says this is racism, bigotry, cruel, and just plain not politically correct. The solution to illegal immigrants is to declare them legal. Presto, problem solved. And that ought to motivate millions more to enter the U.S. illegally.

Foreign policy. Trump states the principle "America first," which was the smear term used to attack those in the Senate and House who resisted our entry into World War II. "America first" always has meant that America's love for its ideals of freedom, human rights, and democratic processes under a constitution does not imply that American men and women must fight and die all over the world when those ideals are threatened. And so, Trump focuses exclusively on the actual attack on Americans by the Islamic State in the Levant (ISIL). To defeat them, he would cooperate with allies such as Russia, Iran, Israel, Iraq, and Turkey. Clinton would oppose head to head the Russian nuclear power in Syria to support "democratic forces" fighting the authoritarian regime. She only reluctantly and with qualifications will even use the term "radical Islamic terrorism."

If you were opposed to Trump at all costs, and Clinton was your horse in the race, would you want the election to be decided based upon the respective, comparative principles and promises of the two candidates? When, in defiance of the positions you deem obviously right, some half of the American people had gone against you, for Trump, what would you do?

The political establishment, intellectual class, and mainstream media are the righteous keepers of the truth, they view any strategy or tactic as fair in winning over hopelessly misled American Trump supporters.

The right thing might be to concede that Americans who disagree with you might elect the next president. But, if you are a politician, part of the "intellectual elite," or part of a media with the mission to battle the judgment of stupid American voters you would change the subject. Abruptly and totally. No more arguing based on positions, where the electorate obviously is hopelessly wrong. Instead, appeal to their "morality," "family values," "decency"—which, by the way, the media always have scorned—to divert them away from the issues and toward debating a decade-old video, released at the perfect time, about an inappropriate private joke.

The art of the politician—and, in this election season, the media and intellectual elites have *become* politicians—is to seize the emotions of the voter on the premise emotions if raw enough always will prevail over reason. Isn't the art of the voter, then, to hear the issues, the principles of the candidate, through the nigh-irresistible siren song of sex, scandal, and righteous scolding?

Penetrating that fog, we see that Republican Party nominee Donald J. Trump wins hands-down on the issues. He defies the Washington establishment and all its cumbrous constituencies—from Greenpeace to the National Educational Association to Black Lives Matter (as a symbol of the movement to create a sense of white tribal/collective guilt).

On the issues, Donald Trump is the candidate to interrupt the momentum of American decline. He is the monkey wrench in the doomsday machine of business as usual. Electing Trump will put the premises of American fatalism—global warming, socialized medicine, abandonment of American exceptionalism, collective white guilt, "redistribution" over production of wealth—on the defensive.

The "truths" assumed by the mighty constituencies for Federal Reserve inflation, for EPA attack on fossil fuels, for the religion of publiceducation spending, and for cutting the defense budget to bolster the welfare state will have to make their case in the glaring spotlight of skepticism. Those lobbies opposed a Trump presidency by even trick in the book because they assumed their causes were beyond questioning. If Trump is elected, they no longer will be Washington insiders who enjoy that assumption.

From the start, that has been Trump's appeal and swept away the field of Republicans competing for the nomination. An outsider, who never has been a politician, who is entirely of the private sector, who never has been submerged in the suffocating politics of identity and its countless oppressed groups, could arrive in Washington, DC, in January 2017, and none of the anointed "players" would be invited to the glitzy inauguration parties. They could stand in the rain along Pennsylvania Avenue and cheer, or weep, like other Americans.

Published October 16, 2016, in *The Savvy Street.*

Chapter 8

The Politics of Women's Hysteria

Why don't millions of American women, including some dearest to me, realize—even now—that Hillary Clinton and her operatives are (at least figuratively) toasting themselves on how they manipulated American women in this election? Personally, I bet they are laughing out loud and doing high fives. Hillary has a ghastly, triumphant smile when she has put one over on her audience.

But I am risking losing your attention, and I value it, so let us turn to cases, facts, and principles. Since at least the beginnings of the Victorian era, women have been portrayed—stereotyped—as susceptible to emotional appeals, suckers for tugging at their heart-strings, and as

susceptible to that vague, and frankly insulting, diagnosis of "hysteria."

The Clinton campaign has counted on that being true, with astonishing success, to turn around this campaign. A private conversation between two men in the studio of a soap opera is taped without their permission or knowledge, essentially by accident ('a hot mic"), and 11 years later it is illicitly released to time exactly with the crucial debates held, supposedly, to permit the American people to choose their next president.

Donald Trump apologizes for loose lips a decade earlier and declares it does not represent who he is. The commenters, interrupting him virtually as he speaks, hasten to declare this an insincere apology. The heads nod in unison across all channels: No, no. On behalf of all American women, we do *not* accept this apology.

From that time, the mass media has no objective—not discussion of political principles, not America's economy, not America's place in the world—but to run and repeat the "groping" story. In the glare of worldwide publicity, several women emerge for a moment on the world stage and are declared courageous heroines by claiming that a decade or more ago Donald Trump "touched them inappropriately" with no witnesses. All the time, they never came forward or complained. There is no other record. There is no way for Mr. Trump to defend himself but to deny what they assert. But he is not innocent until proven guilty; in the press, there is another standard of justice: once accused, you are dead. The new American spirit of justice; tell your kids about that, ladies.

And so, for weeks, the story is the only topic in America's leader of the press, *The New York Times*, where now there is no more "news" on the front page, only feature stories and links to opinion pieces about "groping." The *Times* has succeeded; all of America is *groping* toward 'freedom, truth, and the American way' in this election.

The Smear and Its Target

Well, what about Trump in all this? It has been said that no smear can stick if its object does not lend it credence. By that standard, there seldom has been a more promising target of a smear than Mr. Trump. He is a viscerally aggressive fighter, lashing out when personally attacked, mocking his attackers, jouncing and jiggling and gesturing on stage against his detractors. He is not polished, not "cool," in the Marshall McLuhan sense; he is not politic. His body language is the fighter who raises his clenched fists in response to any insulting personal attack During a campaign when private actions, emails, discussions are the coinage of effective attack, one tape shows Mr. Trump saying that in high school he loved to fight, including with fists. It shows in his campaign.

And so, the long-planned smear attack by Hillary Clinton and her operatives does the trick. In a few weeks, the women of America in their millions are displaying peak "fight or flight" behavior. The valid video of offensive Trump talk in 2005, for which he apologized, is seamlessly attached to "the groped women" incidents, which he denies utterly, and the campaign for the U.S. Presidency flips from Clinton and Trump running neck-and-neck in the polls to Clinton with an impressive lead that Trump closes but never has overcome.

Tens of millions of women of America have focused their attention exclusively on the "pussy tape" and the "groping" saga. They have done so under pressure of a concerted, almost unprecedented media brainwashing campaign to stir up their emotions, their resentments, their fears—their hysteria.

The phenomenon is so strong that it seems possible that the election has been decided by the reaction of America women to "the pussy tapes." In recent weeks, Clinton has pulled well ahead of Trump, from approximately equal; Trump is now the underdog. If so, those women have lived up to the stereotype of the woman who does not venture into the realm of ideas, the economy, and foreign policy; she is captive of her emotional nature, her sensitivity to being slighted, her cry to be heard, taken seriously, respected, viewed as equal.

The Politics of Manipulation

Those are serious demands, assertions of self-respect, but now have been 100 percent co-opted by the Politics of Manipulation. Hillary in public, taking the "high road," talks of her children and grandchildren and how we are voting for their future; she simply cannot mention them often enough. Women. Their feelings. All about family.

Meanwhile, her operatives, undercover and underground, have spent more than a year and millions of dollars preparing for the dirtiest campaign ever run in America. Recently Wikileaks, for example, showed that the "Miss Piggy" attack on Mr. Trump during the debates, asserting that Mr. Trump verbally prodded a Miss Universe winner to fight to keep her title, when it was about to be withdrawn, was researched, twisted, and held for release for more than a year. That's right, a highly paid Clinton agent developed the campaign's book of dirty tricks, including this one, and the Clinton campaign held it more than a year to be ready for use in a debate. That is some impressive plotting to gain power by any means.

What is dismaying to me, on the most personal level, is that the 2016 U.S. Presidential election campaign successfully manipulates American women to a degree I have never witnessed. I wonder if many of them, seized with righteous anger at the "pussy tapes," can cite Mr. Trump's positions on the economy and employment, the environmentalist assault on American energy production, the $2.0 trillion annual drag of Obama-era regulation on the economy, the Trump tax cuts to flip all incentives on U.S. companies toward remaining in America, the Trump "Contract with American Citizens" to fight for freedom, including repealing Obama Care, or the Trump pledge to support schools of choice and charter schools to break the stranglehold of the failing public school monopoly?

I am only one man, of course, and what I witness at first hand is limited. The intelligent, educated, sensitive, highly-confident women I know all are for Clinton and all seem motivated by "pussy tape" politics.

In addition, there is a decided focus on Trump the "bully," on Trump as insensitive to the handicapped, on Trump as unpolished, impolitic, and grating.

He seems to be that, at times, but I see no indication that women in my admittedly limited circle could cite many Trump positions (apart from "the wall") on the issues—in essence, for limited government, more choice for individuals—versus Clinton—in every area for more government power, less freedom of individual action, pledge of managing our lives to make them better.

It is a sad spectacle because the Liberal-Left intellectuals, academics, commentators, reporters, and media columnists support Clinton because of her unflagging, dogmatic advocacy of government control over every area of life at the expense of American freedom—of what remains of free-market capitalism. BUT: when it comes to their columns, comments, and grand-standing TV displays of high moral dudgeon, they speak only of the "pussy tape" themes.

They have discovered that that is where the decisive electoral majority for Clinton is to be found. Get those millions of women voting their anger at men, and their fear, and the entire Trump attack on the socialist-drifting, interventionist-welfare statist, anti-free-market Clinton program can be defeated—defeated without ever discussing it.

Published November 1, 2016, in *The Savvy Street*.

Chapter 9

The Not-So-Complex Case of Comey

As soon as I walked into the kitchen, this morning, where my wife had the TV on, I heard a Hillary Clinton "surrogate" attacking FBI Director James Comey for informing Congressional leaders that he was re-opening the criminal investigation of Clinton for possible illegal handling of classified information to which she was privy as Secretary of State.

All through breakfast, struggling to enjoy my frittata, sausages, and croissants (my wife does not skimp), I saw fulminating faces pitching the Clinton line: What Comey had done was unfair, unethical, unprecedented; he had no idea what was in the emails; they probably were the same emails the FBI already had seen; "incomprehensible" to re-open the investigation; the FBI must release all emails instantly; the FBI had created an "intolerable situation…" The big faces filling the screen sweated with moral intensity.

Just to give you a preview of what is to come:

Senate Minority Leader Harry Reid (D) back in June, when Comey announced he was closing the investigation of Clinton, declaring that although she had been "extremely careless" with classified information, there was not enough evidence at that time to prosecute her, declared: "No one can question the integrity of this man."

Harry Reid, yesterday, when the appearance of a mountain of possible new evidence convinced Comey that he must keep his pledge to Congress, made under oath back in July, to reopen the investigation if new possible new evidence appeared, wrote in a public letter to

Comey: "Your actions…have demonstrated a disturbing double standard for the treatment of sensitive information, with what appears to be a clear intent to aid one political party over another." Just to be clear, he added, "… you may have broken the law."

In just three months, the Director of the FBI, appointed by President Obama and approved by Reid's Senate by 93 to 1, has gone from being a man of integrity to a political hack and quite possibly a criminal. What *other* explanation can there be except possibly that Harry Reid is an unprincipled liar who will say anything for the sake of politics? That is plausible…

Why did Comey re-open the Clinton email investigation, now"? Answer: On Thursday, an FBI team investigating the Anthony Weiner text-messaging sex case in New York City, got in touch with the FBI team that had investigated the Clinton private email server case and the possibility of the Secretary of State having mishandled classified documents. The Weiner team said: We found lots of emails that seem relevant to the Clinton case (after 9/11, separate FBI teams and other federal investigators are supposed to share information, remember?).

Why did Comey re-open the case at all? Answer: On Friday, the day after the FBI Clinton-investigation team got this information, they went to Director Comey with it. He examined the information and ascertained that it seemed "pertinent" to the Clinton investigation. These were materials apparently never seen in the investigation of Clinton that the FBI concluded in July.

Why did Comey release the information that he was re-opening the investigation? Answer: He did not release it publicly. Deciding that the materials warranted re-opening the Clinton investigation, he informed the chairmen of eight Congressional committees, along with their vice chairman–i.e., Republican and Democratic leaders of all the committees—that he had found evidence warranting a re-opening of the investigation.

Why did he release the information at all? After all, as soon as they received the letter from Comey, some of the chairmen of the Congressional committees leaked it to the press. Answer: Comey told his FBI staff and the Justice Department that ordinarily the FBI would not release even to Congress news that an investigation was being opened and, in particular, the Justice Department 'guidance" was against releasing such information affecting some public official 60 days before an election. But, said Comey, this was special.

What special factors could justify Comey's notifying Congressional chairmen of the investigation, when the Justice Department had a precedent—although not a law or regulation– against it? Answer: This was not a new investigation. The FBI had been investigating the Clinton private email server and possible security leaks of classified information up until July 1 of this year. What is more, also under oath, he had testified that if any new information came to light, he would review it, a.k.a., re-open the investigation.

There was immense pressure on the FBI to close the investigation because Secretary of State Clinton was a candidate for the U.S. Presidency. Under intense criticism for a "cover-up," Comey nevertheless testified to the Congressional committees in July that the FBI was closing the investigation. Hillary Clinton's handling of the situation had been "extremely careless" and had lacked judgment, he testified, but there was not enough evidence to recommend prosecuting her. And so, on this most recent Friday, Comey was re-opening an investigation that he had testified under oath he was closing. What is more, also under oath, he had testified that if any new information came to light, he would review it, a.k.a., reopen the investigation. As Yahoo News reports: "Comey was further compelled to review the documents based on two factors: the volume of documents and his commitment under oath to Congress to review 'any new and substantial information,' the source also said."

But didn't the Justice Department tell him not to inform Congress of re-opening the investigation? Answer: Comey checked in with the Justice Department on the matter and was advised that the Department did not inform Congress when opening criminal investigations of public officials less than 60 days before an election. And, as stated, he replied: This is a new investigation. I testified to Congress I was closing it and under oath that I would re-open if warranted. Now, I am re-opening it and feel obligated to inform the Congressional chairs and vice chairs. In addition, that July decision to close the investigation had a very significant effect on the Presidential election, so the public deserves to know that that decision has been reversed.

So, the Justice Department did advise Comey not to inform Congress? Answer: Apparently, that is right. (By the way, Comey is not unaware of Justice Department policies and practices. Before President Obama appointed him FBI Director, Comey was #2 at the Justice Department.) Comey gave the reasons explained above and went ahead. The rest is speculation. Did the top Obama appointees at Justice, knowing this announcement would be political dynamite, want to distance themselves? And did Comey let them do that? (He is sort of famous as a tough-minded "I will take all responsibility" kind of lawman. But no one knows.)

But isn't it true that all Hillary Clinton and the talking-face legion on Sunday morning TV are demanding is that the FBI release all information and reach and announce a decision before November 8 and the election? Answer: Yes. They have literally zero other options. Typically, someone under criminal investigation (Chapter 18. U.S. Code) by the FBI is not able to demand that the FBI keep to a certain timetable and high public officials have no different rights in that regard. But let's get real: this is a candidate for the U.S. Presidency and a gigantic amount is at stake. Apparently, there are hundreds of thousands of emails on the computer that a top Clinton aide shared with her then-husband, Anthony Weiner. The questions about each email will be, at least as I understand it: Does this convey classified information? If so, was that information classified when transmitted? Is any of this information now known to have leaked to foreign sources? And did Secretary of State Clinton knowingly and intentionally share classified information or was this more "extremely careless mishandling"?

But should a case like this, coming up just 11 days before a U.S. Presidential election, be permitted to have potentially momentous consequences for the outcome? Answer: In one sense, this question merely rephrases earlier questions: Why did this come up now? (New evidence came to light.) Why announce it? (It already was a prominent factor in the election, this was an update.) The July testimony of FBI Director Comey to Congress appeared to take the issue of potential criminal charges against Clinton out of the election; the new evidence brought it back in and the public had a right to know. Will it, though, affect the outcome of the election?

Just two days after the FBI letter to Congressional chairmen and vice chairmen, the chief impact has been to put the Clinton campaign in full attack mode; in the context, one cannot fault them. What else can they do? The "message" is awful, so portray the messenger as politically motivated, in violation of accepted practices, bearing a message of no importance, and breaking the law. The first polls reflecting impact of the new information suggest that one-third of registered voters now are "less inclined" to vote for Clinton. Another poll suggests that Clinton and Trump are neck-and-neck in the race. Against that is the factor rightly cited by Mrs. Clinton that most voters have made up their minds about

"the emails."

But what will be the upshot on November 8 and beyond? Answer: Excuse me, you may be confusing me with the Oracle at Delphi. I am just a very confused and conflicted American voter. I am ever so grateful to solicit your thoughts about all this.

Published November 5, 2016, in *The Savvy Street*.

Chapter 10

"Less Is More" in U.S. Presidents, Too

When it comes to choosing our next President, "Less is more" is a kind of corollary of the golden rule "that government is best that governs least." This comparison began to take shape in my mind over many weeks of consulting with my basic principles and values about the candidacy of Donald J. Trump versus Hillary R. Clinton—a decision Americans must make next Tuesday.

Now, I see it almost in terms of a list. What *doesn't* Donald Trump have? We could play with such a list, of course, beginning with his lack of a competent hair stylist, but my purpose, here, is serious.

Trump has no experience in political office. At age 70, his lifelong perspective has been that of a businessman trying to develop major construction projects in one of America's most over-regulated cities, a corporate taxpayer, an investor—but never a politician. He notably is running against Washington as a true outsider.

Trump is just not attuned to identity politics—the sacred—call it, obsessive—cause of politicians as well as those in education, academia, and the media. While Ms. Clinton never speaks without addressing the supposed interests of Whites versus African-Americans and HispanicAmericans, American citizens versus illegal aliens, Blacks versus White law enforcement, gays, lesbians, and transgendered individuals versus other Americans, and women versus men, this perspective seems absent from the thinking of Donald Trump. The only "identity" politics he raises are concerns about some 10-million or more individuals who have entered the United States illegally and so have incentives to avoid legal authority in all areas including taxes, Social Security, law-enforcement, and so on.

Trump has not built his career on any political constituencies— because he has not been in politics. He is not beholden to the hugely powerful teachers' unions, the giant business lobbies such as the Chamber of Commerce and multi-million-dollar Wall Street donors, labor unions, various industries from energy to high technology, U.S. veterans' groups... Yes, some powerful groups have chosen to back him, including big bucks from the National Rifle Association (a cheap political date, since all they want is no new laws or regulations), veterans' groups (a valid concern of government), and some business interests.

Notably, his support is among white voters without a college education (not sure why that is so important, though); they do not tend to be the source of huge financial contributions.

In fact, Mr. Trump has run a notoriously "cheap" campaign, raising less than half the funds that Ms. Clinton has raised, and he has put tens of millions of his own money into his campaign. No one has bought him and, given his wealth, no one can.

Mr. Trump has not been baptized, as has Ms. Clinton, into the religion of radical environmentalism, with its worship of the "natural" over the science, engineering, technology, and industry that meet the needs of human beings and make possible the economic prosperity that the radical environmentalists view as a threat to the planet. Mr. Trump does not attack environmentalism or deny it; he is reasonable, but just not sold on it as is Hillary Clinton, who lists "global warming" it as the number one threat to our future. His "Contract with America" pledges that on his first day in office he will initiate steps to reclaim from the United Nations the billions our country has handed over to environmentalists. He will focus his environmental program on clear air and clean water.

Mr. Trump does not view regulation as synonymous with the government's power to do good and an automatic answer to any problem in any sector of American life. In fact, as a real-estate developer in New York City, where housing costs are triple and quadruple the rest of America—and still little housing is available—he understands that regulation is simply the "business," the prosperity, the power of bureaucrats. In his "Contract with America," he pledges a rule that for every new regulation proposed two existing regulations must be cut.

Mr. Trump has not run his election with the support of the Republican Party; if he wins, he will not owe the party the slightest obeisance. That is rare, if not unique, in American history. There is one exception to this, and I view it as an important concern. Mr. Trump's most fervent, numerous supporters include many Christian evangelicals who constitute the Republican party "base." As must every candidate to have any chance at the Republican nomination, Mr. Trump had to pay lip service to "the right to life." We know and his enemies have said again and again that that is not his real position. Nor can I recall ever hearing him emphasize it in speeches or the debates. What Mr. Trump did do is name Michael Pence his vice-presidential candidate and Mr. Pence is a serious Christian and leader of the right-to-life movement. I view this as a negative for Mr. Trump.

Mr. Trump, his enemies will whole-heartedly agree, lacks any sense of the "politically correct" (that is not true, just listen to precampaign Trump, who can be sensitive, politic, and strictly correct) in his campaign rhetoric or concerns. In 2009, President Obama had an opportunity to appoint an associate justice of the Supreme Court and chose Sonia Maria Sotomayor, thereby crossing himself by touching both "woman" and "Hispanic heritage." We will see how she votes on the latest celebrated case to be accepted by the court: the right of transgendered individuals to decide on the public restroom of their choice. A Black President appoints a female Hispanic-American member of the Supreme Court to decide a case on transgendered individuals. Does that deliberately provocative characterization prove anything? No, of course not. But when Ms. Clinton in the debates was asked how she would make appointments to the Supreme Court, she answered with a long list of identity-politics concerns. She never mentioned the U.S. Constitution. Mr. Trump was succinct. He would appoint justices to uphold the U.S. Constitution, he said.

Mr. Trump brings scant foreign policy experience to the White House. As a businessman, he has considerable familiarity with the trade regulations, foreign competition, currency wars, and tariff changes that affect American enterprise in a global economy. In that area, he has definite ideas and it is not clear if they aim at "fair trade" or protectionism. It has been pointed out, again and again, that his goals can be achieved without protectionism; but there is no guarantee he will act that way. In other fields of foreign policy, Mr. Trump has no experience, but, then, neither did Ronald Reagan, who, based on clear principles and firm commitments, ushered in the end of the Soviet evil empire. Jimmy Carter had no foreign policy experience and was a disaster; Bill Clinton, too, had no special foreign policy experience. Nor did George W. Bush or Barrack Obama. Hillary Clinton, as secretary of state for eight years, has a great deal of foreign policy experience, foreign travel, and familiarity with foreign governments and leaders.

Mr. Trump has not the slightest indebtedness to the media (laugh, here), nor incentive to heed their exhortations, or take seriously their urgings and recommendations. Sitting in the Oval Office, on a future morning, weighing decisions on policy, pity the obtuse aide or advisor who says, "Well, the *New York Times* urges that you… and CNN would editorialize in your favor if you…" If Trump becomes our next President, it will despite the worst the mainstream media can do. How upset will President Trump be if the *New York Times* reports that children are having bad dreams about his global warming policy?

Trump is not stuck with the Affordable Care Act. He has said that if elected he will seek to repeal it; his alternative is tax-exempt medical savings accounts. As the most significant single legislative measure achieved by the Obama administration, there is no way Clinton will change Obamacare. It sounds as though she intends to fix its problems by extending it toward a fully socialist system.

Trump, to say the very least, will not ride into the White House on a wave of anti-gun, gun-control fervor—but Clinton will. Both are unequivocal. Trump will uphold the Second Amendment; Clinton will uphold her own version of the Second Amendment.

Trump will not bring into the White House a spouse with an admitted record of using the most powerful position in the world to seduce a 22-year-old White House intern. With Bill back in the White House what *will* be the special precautions to protect the youngest, most vulnerable women on the staff? Maybe he could be limited to kissing them inappropriately and on his birthday groping one.

Well, despite best efforts, this list has degenerated to the level of a *New York Times* editorial on the campaign, so I will stop here.

Published November 5, 2016, in *The Savvy Street*.

Chapter 11

The Media Stages the First "Post-Modern" Election

> "*Postmodernism became the leading intellectual movement in the late twentieth century. It has replaced modernism, the philosophy of the Enlightenment.*
> *For modernism's principles of objective reality, reason, and individualism, it has substituted its own precepts of relative feeling, social construction, and group-ism.*
> *This substitution has now spread to major cultural institutions such as education, journalism, and the law, where it manifests itself as race and gender politics, advocacy journalism, political correctness, multiculturalism, and the rejection of science and technology.*"
>
> Dr. Stephen Hicks, Professor of Philosophy, Rockford University

Here is a tip for you. When a person's beliefs, or a cultural phenomenon (such as a Presidential election), or an interpretation of reality (such as the mass media analysis and grossly wrong prediction of the election) seems incomprehensible to you—not just wrong, but unfathomable—it is because it proceeds from fundamental philosophical premises you have not identified.

Tuesday night, election eve 2016 in the United States, I was watching PBS Channel 13's coverage of the unfolding election and its results. The panelists were intelligent and highly experienced and sophisticated, intent on understanding what was happening, seemingly open to being surprised (not much choice there!), and, in the end, able to indulge in some humility as they sat stunned and acutely embarrassed at the election's sweeping triumph for

Republican Donald J. Trump over Democrat Hillary R. Clinton. I had not expected as much and admire their performance—and that, too, is part of this mystery.

In the months leading up to Election Day, the repeated national polls by CNN, the *Wall Street Journal*, the *Los Angeles Times*, Rasmussen, and a dozen other organizations reported, week after week, that Hillary Clinton was in the lead. The size of that lead fluctuated, certainly, and polls tightened toward the election, but on election eve the respected site "Real Clear Politics" gave Clinton a 2.2 percent average lead over Trump. (One poll only, International Business Daily/TRIPP, showed Trump leading and, to their credit, some media sources pointed out that IBD/TRIPP had been most accurate in the past. Well, they did it again.)

Hillary Clinton had been in the race for the Democratic presidential nomination for months, against openly socialist candidate Senator Bernard Sanders (D.-VT)—a race the media covered with a respectful attitude (by media standards)—when New York City billionaire builder, Atlantic City casino pioneer, and, more recently, TV personality, Donald J. Trump, crashed the Republican Presidential nomination gala that already featured some 15 or more contenders.

Although he never held public office, Trump had been testing the waters for more than a decade in both parties, on the state level as well as federal. He tested the idea of being a candidate of the Reform Party as early as 1999. He was an active Democrat for a while. But by June 16, 2015, he seemed to have committed himself and at Trump Towers on legendary Fifth Avenue in New York City, he entered the race for the Republican nomination for President.

Postmodern Journalism and "Identity Politics"

In that speech, on the first day of his candidacy, Trump— knowingly or unknowingly, perhaps someday we will know—threw himself, like an airborne fullback, straight into the path of postmodern politics and, above all, *postmodern journalism*. And that explains the squalid level of campaigning that followed: the media's almost exclusive focus on racial and sexual antagonism and its portrait of the country as endlessly divided and divisive. The result was rising levels of personal animosity among voters and near certainty that Mr. Trump would be rejected as racist, xenophobic, misogynist, unqualified for office, temperamentally unfit—swept away by the force of minimal American decency.

It also explains Ms. Clinton's marathon record of spending more time on a single meme, "Stronger Together," and inventing more ways to say, 'all of us," than any candidate in the history of U.S. elections. The remainder of the time she spent ridiculing, demeaning, and demonizing her opponent.

This obsessive focus of the campaign on group identity and antagonism was the creation of America's postmodernist reporters, editors, commentators, TV hosts, and public intellectuals. It was synergistic with the Clinton campaign, which had spent more than a year researching and preparing attacks on Mr. Trump–all based on "identity politics"—and waiting for the moment to unleash them. But … the media needed no such added stimulus; they manufactured the public image of Donald Trump that the Clinton campaign then propagated, only to have her words reported by the press … and so on, and on.

Today, the "narrative" of the campaign—its meaning, supposed central conflict, and characters—created by the media—is causing the intense post-election rage, depression, and righteous indignation. We see Yale undergraduate girls sprawled together, weeping; heavily racially accented riots on both coasts; internet posts by frightened women; and columns in the foreign press on our "racist, fascist" new President. The press eagerly reports this, shaking its collective head, again and again, and explaining: Well this is what happens when the people … and then repeating their own manufactured version of what the election of Trump meant.

"The wall"

Throwing his hat into the ring on June 16, 2015, Mr. Trump pointed out the most obvious new fact of American life, felt in towns from the tip of Long Island (my town, East Hampton) to California, from the State of Washington to Arizona and Texas, visible every day, on every street. in every business: new immigrants from across America's southern border, including an estimated 11.0 million Mexicans and others who entered the country illegally, beginning their residency by breaking the law and with every incentive to avoid contact with the police, IRS, Social Security, and other authorities—illegally employed, often paying no taxes or Social Security, using services such as schools and health care facilities supported by local, state, and federal taxes.

That was (and is) the reality in the face of Americans during a decade of agonizingly slow recovery from the financial panic and crash of 2008, a recovery of employment at a staggering price in new federal debt (doubled during the Obama years to $19 trillion), and Federal Reserve distortion of the financial markets (near-zero interest rates for nine years). It was a time during which high school and college graduates had one of the highest unemployment rates in U.S. history; the unemployment rate among young African-Americans was catastrophic. In cities and towns across America, illegal immigrants, paid off the books, costing their employers no benefits, held millions of entry level jobs.

Appealing to the principle of the rule of law, consistently, not selectively, Mr. Trump said that a Trump administration would halt illegal immigration, reverse it by returning illegal immigrants to Mexico, and prevent new millions from pouring across the southern border by completing the barrier started decades ago and *extended during the Obama administration*. He went on to say what had been frequently reported, and that Americans knew, that the Mexican government was alleged to have exploited the porous border to drive criminals— "murders, rapists, and drug dealers"—out of Mexico and into the United States.

Later, this was pointed out. Mr. Trump did not refer to Mexicans in general who were coming across the border, but to those Mexico was "sending" across the border. It made no difference, of course. From that moment, America's foremost newspapers, magazines, and radio and television news programs went into irreversible, unrelenting opposition to the Trump candidacy. Trump had identified a postmodernist grouping (Mexicans and other Latinos who entered the country illegally) and taken a political stand against it.

If you have followed the entire 18-month Trump rise in America, winning over the wide field of candidates for the Republican nomination, then winning the 2016 election race against Hillary Clinton, you know that during those 18 months nothing caused the mass media in America to waver from its attack on Donald Trump as "xenophobic," "racist," and "misogynist." There is scant evidence for any of this and all the most prominent examples—except for the "pussy tapes"—were manufactured by the press.

Trump as Postmodernist "Oppressor"

Postmodernism in an individual, group, profession, or culture is the underlying premise that there is no fixed, objective reality and thus no objective truth. In social relations, it is the struggle between the oppressed and the oppressing groups that explains the meaning of our actions. Our significance is not as individuals, but as members of a racial, ethnic, economic, and sexual group. The narrative of the press, with all its breathtaking episodes, was created to place candidate Trump solidly among the oppressors.

The Trump candidacy began to be defined, during its opening press conference, as an appeal to "working class," non-college educated, white, racist, misogynist Americans against the oppressed classes. And so. this first "postmodern" U.S. electoral campaign became a treasure hunt for real or manufactured evidence of this hypothesis.

Media attacks mounted to become daily inventive smears, not only on opinion pages, but run as front-page stories (it was not uncommon for the *New York Times* to start a dozen anti-Trump "stories" daily on its front page). How to find so many? Well, take the headline, "Times Reporter Says Her Daughter Having Bad Dreams about Trump." Or a story on half-a-dozen teenaged daughters of "Times" reporters, and how their "body image" had been affected by Trump's remarks.

Astoundingly, while being made the greatest scare and hate figure in the American media since Richard Nixon—many whispered Hitler— Mr. Trump did not shrink back or lose heart; he swept across America defiant, his rallies surged in size, and—not insignificantly—neither the press not anyone else could talk about anything else.

Soon came the big "Trump University" scandal, alleging that a "university"—really a program—created by Trump for aspiring businessmen and New York "deal makers"—was a fraud. Till that moment, there had been widespread praise and endorsement of Trump University. But *National Geographic*, you know, reported a poll showing that 77 percent of Americans believe there are signs that intelligent aliens have visited Earth. It was not difficult to find a dozen or so New Yorkers to testify to their discontent with the University.

Also, a lawsuit had been filed against the University and this became the new media rage.

I will be brief because the story is well known. With the press united in attacking Trump University as a failure and fraud and, thus, attacking Mr. Trump as an incompetent businessman, Mr. Trump said that his lawyers felt that the judge in the case was biased against the defense (Trump University). He said he wasn't sure why, but the judge was of Mexican heritage, said Trump, and "I am going to build that wall." Given the widespread anger in Mexico and among Mexican Americans at the proposed wall, said Trump, the judge might not be able to decide the Trump case fairly and should recuse himself.

I submit to you that this example alone fails to suggest that Mr. Trump is "racist" and it is one of very few even cited. House Speaker Paul Ryan inexplicably joined the critics—well, not inexplicably, he saw in media reporting of this incident the coming tidal wave of media exploitation of the race card. Another major charge against Trump was that decades ago one Trump building in New York City was charged with exclusion based on race; Mr. Trump and his organization defended themselves. No guilt was admitted or demonstrated, no fine paid. It is notable that the Trump organization controls hundreds of thousands of rental apartments in New York City and no other case is cited.

In fact, as a New Yorker familiar with its news, personalities, and rumors, I know that until the election no charges related to race, no rumors, surrounded Mr. Trump.

One other media frenzy concludes the race issue. As bombs and gun attacks by Islamic Americans shook the country, as did the mass murders by Islamic radicals in Paris, Mr. Trump suggested that the United States should halt immigration from such ISIS hot spots as Syria until "we know what is going on." His proposal was to be sure that the vetting of new entrants from these countries was effective in identifying the killers that ISIS vowed again and again to send.

And that is the whole case for "racist" candidate Trump. In literally thousands of hours of solemn TV talk shows, and thousands of media stories, postmodern "advocacy" journalism has fulfilled its mission: to crusade not for truth and balance but to expose and oppose the "oppressor." A word or gesture at a Trump rally, the endorsement by the legendary "David Duke" of the Ku Klux Klan—instantly repudiated by Trump—and endless interviews with African-Americans—created the impression over months that the entire Trump movement was aimed at racially motivated white Americans. And, said star *New York Times* columnist, Paul Krugman, it is not just explicit racism but "dog whistle" messages from Trump that are picked up by his "white nationalist" supporters. Just in case nothing that Trump said could be demonstrated to be racist.

As Trump supporters increased and Trump swept the entire field of Republican contenders to take the nomination, and gathered support as the election approached, the press congratulated themselves for being right. White, "non-college educated" (this repeated endlessly), middle American voters must not care that Trump was racist. Obviously! The media had told them over and over a million times in stories, editorials, testimonials, panel discussions, and photographs that their man was a bigot. They must be racist, too!

What Trump Advocated

On his campaign Web site, and in every speech I heard (none in person), Mr. Trump set forth positions characterized by one political principle and goal: reduce government intervention and involvement in the lives of Americans and view all Americans as equal but none as having special rights.

■   Halt all new regulation-making and begin to deregulate. Regulation is now an estimated $2.0 trillion a year drag on the economy; some 60 major new regulations, at an annual cost of $670 billion, were added to that total during the Obama administration.

■   Deregulate and encourage the American energy industry, including all fossil fuels, in which a couple years ago, for the first time in history, America became the number one producer in the world—fulfilling a decades-long promise of government to make America energy independent of foreign authoritarian producers.

■   Stop investing billions in research and remediation of so-called "global warming" and "climate change." Trump is on record as reasonable on this issue, and, of course, acknowledges the phenomenon of global warming (as does virtually every scientist), but, like many scientists, does not see any compelling evidence that global warming/climate change represents a long-term threat to the planet.

He would claw back from the United Nations billions of U.S. dollars spent on this crusade. During the Obama Administration, more new regulations were imposed by the Environmental Protection Agency than all other government departments combined. And most arose from the mindset of the Greenpeace radical environmentalists, who are driven by ideology, not science.

■   Reduce taxes on corporations from an average of 25 to 30 percent to an average of 15 percent, a huge incentive for corporations to remain in the United States, invest more, create more jobs, and bring back enterprises from overseas.

■   Direct new federal money for education to a search for alternatives to the public-school monopoly that for decades has been failing, especially in the inner cities, despite huge new investments. The Trump position mentions schools of choice, charter schools, and vouchers—all of which would empower parents, especially those trapped with inner city schools, to become involved in deciding where to educate their children.

■   Uphold the Second Amendment right to bear arms with appropriate screening to spot individuals who cannot be trusted with the responsibility of firearms.

■   Appoint Supreme Court justices who will uphold the *U.S. Constitution* in their decisions instead of using appointments to meet racial, ethnic, and sex quotas and seat justices who will view the Constitution as a non-legislative instrument of social engineering. Not one of these positions is "progressive"—increasing government power to enforce collectivist ideals such as "social justice," "fairness," an end to "oppression," "multiculturalism," "globalism," "green peace," "equal pay for women," "national health care," "social democracy," "animal rights," and totally tax-supported higher education.

Not that Mr. Trump explicitly opposes these utopian hopes; he just never indicates interest in them. Nor are they the ideals of most of the Americans across the great swathe of the country between the two coasts who elected him on November 8. Their ideals are private initiative, success earned by work, wealth as a consequence of effort, the unquestioned value of increasing national prosperity, embracing new technology and admiration for "progress," individual reonsibility, responsibility for family, education as virtually synonymous with opportunity, contributing to community, reverence for the rule of law, religious tolerance, moral judgment as pertaining to individuals not groups, pride in American ideals and the American example as a beacon to the world, American self interest in the world, and reliance on strength to defend America.

When Mr. Trump blazoned on his ensign, "Make America Great Again," his supporters interpreted this to mean the restoration, protection, and renewal of such ideals. They did not think of the ideals of progressivism that tend to be engendered in the big cities on America's east and west coasts where the print and broadcast media, entertainment industry, leading universities, major foundations, and large "alternative lifestyle" communities tend to be heavily concentrated.

The news media, once a matter of a daily newspaper, the six o'clock news, and a handful of wide-circulation news magazines, now dominate the airwaves and internet 24 hours a day. Owned by huge corporate conglomerates resulting from years of consolidation, they field hundreds of thousands of bright, talented, ambitious graduates of the colleges and universities that are the breeding grounds and transmission centers of postmodern philosophy, postmodernism is politics, postmodernism is art, and postmodernism in journalism.

Not entirely consciously—certainly no pacts or conspiracies or cabals shape the vast, varied media of America and the media is not entirely uniform in its views—in 2016 *America's mass media came to cast the election in terms of the very essence of postmodernism: identity politics* and the premise that all political positions reflect the struggle of the oppressors to defeat the struggles of the oppressed. It is an axiom of this view that "people of color," women, immigrant ethnic groups, the poor, gays and lesbians, the physically handicapped, and animals are habitually oppressed. The oppressor is the White race—especially the middle class, the traditional, the male.

Mr. Trump's positions were infrequently mentioned, if at all, and then quickly dismissed; many commentators whose *real* opposition was to those positions, seemed to find it more effective to attack Mr. Trump as bigoted, of dubious character, as emotionally unstable…

I have dealt at least briefly with the charges of racism and xenophobia. An even more explosive charge, because of its "sex appeal" as a news story, was Mr. Trump's treatment of women. It is not too much to say that the single issue that dominated the campaign—at the choice of the media—was the tape leaked by a news television studio of Mr. Trump, some 11 years earlier, in what was a private conversation, accidentally taped without his knowledge, boasting that as a TV celebrity, he found women welcomed his abrupt sexual advances. He put it in the most vulgar way possible, in terms of "grabbing their pussy," and so was launched the "groping" story. The media chose to give nothing in the campaign more attention than this tape, played, quoted, described, and discussed literally hundreds of thousands of time. In this, they indicated the paramountcy of any proof positive of "oppression"—in this case, of course, of women.

It was a "news judgment," which is fair enough, and red meat for audiences, and speaking to their "college educated" peers in the audience, the press evoked a resounding response. This was bedrock postmodernism: the wealthy white male declaring his power over the very genitalia of the oppressed. The media were quick to point out—I recall one African-American panelist shouting it repeatedly—that had Mr. Trump acted on his words it would have been sexual assault, a criminal offense.

No one ever produced any evidence that Mr. Trump had acted on his macho boast, although the media, starting with the powerful reportorial staff of the *New York Times*, made a sustained effort. In the end, some half-dozen women were produced and hailed as heroines, stars, for claiming that Mr. Trump had "touched them inappropriately," but, alas, there were no witnesses and Mr. Trump denied it. Ordinarily, the premise in our justice system is that charges must be proved for there to be guilt, but the journalists understood very well that the rule in the media is "if you are accused, you're dead."

The media smear campaign that followed did not dwell on the numbers but veered from the "New Jersey" story to a fabricated libel of Trump mocking a disabled individual.

The "misogyny" charge got one booster shot. One of the "dumps" of hacked emails from the computer of the Clinton campaign's head, John Podesta—a contribution of the organization WikiLeaks to journalism-byillegal-means throughout the campaign—revealed that more than some year earlier Clinton campaign operatives searched for every possible piece of damaging evidence with which to attack opponents, including Trump. One such discovery was a tape 20 years ago when Mr. Trump owned the "Miss Universe" franchise. A new Miss Universe from Venezuela, in 1996, Alicia Machado, was being pressured to resign because after winning the prize she gained more than 50 pounds during the period when she was obligated to be displaying her charms around the country.

Mr. Trump did not fire her, however, but went to her rescue. It is fascinating to watch the video of Mr. Trump announcing to reporters and others that Miss Machado was going to be kept on and helped to lose weight. A sensitive, warm, and often humorous Trump introduced the top trainer who had been hired, then said Miss Machado would be working with him daily, and joked with reporters that both he and they could stand to lose some weight, too. He explained that the pressures on the very young Miss Universe candidates were severe and that, after all, many of us react to stress by overeating. It was understandable; obesity was a serious issue in America. Miss Machado is shown sitting next to where Mr. Trump is standing, thanking him, clutching his sleeve, nodding vigorously, and even saying, "You can work out with me anytime, Mr. Trump." Trump smiles, pats her arm, and says, "You're going to do all right."

That tape was not chosen to nail Mr. Trump as a misogynist. Later, reporters were invited back to watch Miss Machado working out, with much laughter and joking. At some point, although it was not recorded, Trump may have been encouraging her to do a few more sit-ups and jokingly said, "Come on, Miss Piggy, you can do it." There is no documentation of the moment.

Fast forward two full decades to one of the three prime-time Presidential debates with a huge national audience. Suddenly, Clinton is relating how Trump called Miss Universe a 'fat shaming' name, "Miss Piggy," then turns to Mr. Trump and says, "She has a *name*, Donald!" Trump at first looks mystified, asking, "Where did you get…"

Then, apparently, he remembers back 20 years and starts to say, "But I saved her position …" It is too late, of course. Mr. Trump has assaulted another woman, this time verbally. And the oppressor has been insensitive to yet another oppressed group: the overweight.

The Clinton campaign had found Miss Machado, who had left her native Venezuela to become a U.S. citizen. She now recalled that she had been mortified, terrified, when Mr. Trump called her "Miss

Piggy." She had never forgotten it, she was traumatized. For years afterward, she said, she had had "eating disorders." Except that, in a much earlier interview, she had said that in the *run-up* to the Miss Universe campaign she had suffered from "anorexia and bulimia" and added "Most of us [contestants] did."

The story blazes through the media, with Miss Machado as a symbol of an oppressed woman–could be anyone's daughter, you know— and, by the campaign's end, she is traveling through Florida from rally to rally with Mrs. Clinton to tell heavily Hispanic audiences that for women Mr. Trump would be a terrifying President.

If you have not had enough of this, by now, you have an admirably strong stomach. But anyone who followed the 2016 Presidential election knows—whatever his or her perspective—that "groping," and "Miss Piggy," came virtually to define the campaign, including the three Presidential debates. Mrs. Clinton never went more than a few minutes without referring to them, always in the postmodernist context of identity politics and oppression.

The Strange Tale of the Disabled Reporter

Just one more refrain must be mentioned. On the basis of one incident, the media and Clinton campaign added to the characterization of Mr. Trump that he "made fun of the disabled." Mr. Trump never seems to have had the imagination to foresee how his actions could be used against him and provide priceless footage for his opponents. At a rally on November 21, 2015, Mr. Trump said that he recalled reading in the press that on the night of 9/11 attacks Arab-Americans were cheering the attack on roofs in New Jersey. He said he knew it was not "politically correct" to say so, but that is the report he read.

All major news outlets immediately denied there ever had been such a report. The *Washington Post* did a "fact check" just to confirm this. And then, oh heaven! It turned out that a *Washington Post* story by Serge Kovaleski, on September 18, 2001, had reported the story and that police had arrested the demonstrators. Oh my, and the *Post* had just done a "fact check" of all media and reported finding nothing.

Washington Post agents, finding Kovaleski now working at the *New York Times*, pressed him and he backtracked on his story, saying, at least as quoted: "I certainly do not remember anyone saying that thousands or even hundreds of people were celebrating. That was not the case, as best as I can remember…"

True, Mr. Trump did say "thousands and thousands" and that was not confirmed (a September 16, 2001, news video merely said "swarms"). But this had nothing to do with the media smear campaign that followed. That campaign did not dwell on the numbers but veered from the "New Jersey" story to a fabricated libel of Trump as mocking a disabled individual. Back to "identity politics." This is how it happened.

Confronted with this seeming recantation of the *Post* story, at a rally in South Carolina, Mr. Trump recounted the above explanation and, in one of his unrestrained moments, pantomimed the flustered reporter protesting "No, no, no—I never said that." Mr. Trump brushed his hands up and down, laughing at the reporter desperately denying the charge of having written his own story, and, just for good measure, made a quite funny face of the horrified reporter.

It so happened that Mr. Kovaleski has a disability, one hand frozen in a curled-over position. Some enterprising photographer took a single frozen frame from the entire video of Mr. Trump's antics, at the precise moment his hand seemed to be curled down; the photographer then set this beside a photograph of the reporter, standing in the same pose as Mr. Trump, his hand curled down. There you go, a headline story: Trump mocks the disability of reporter. It would not have resonated so well without the rather undignified display of jiggling by Mr. Trump—he is the opposite of "cool" in the Marshall McLuhan sense—which was shown thousands of times with new captions like "What will we tell our children?"

But, it effectively diverted all attention from the *Washington Post's* ridiculous "fact finding" report, missing its own story, and from Mr. Trump's point about Arab-Americans in New Jersey cheering the attack on the World Trade Center. I have recounted this at length to document a major campaign "theme" and make the point that the postmodern journalist does not consider facts, nor objectivity–in which he does not believe–but only the impact of the "right" worldview.

The narrative of the press, both fed and adopted by Hillary Clinton, was complete. *Trump the racist, sexist, misogynist, xenophobic ridiculer of the disabled.*

Published November 18, 2016, in *The Savvy Street.*

Chapter 12

America Votes Postmodernism: No, Trump: Yes

"During the last forty years, we have seen such postmodernism come to dominate the humanities in higher education and replace traditional scholarship with puerile analyses cast in terms of race, sex, and economic status. Very recently, this corrupting postmodern technique has been transmitted downward to the mass media."
Dr. Stephen Hicks, Professor of Philosophy, Rockford University

The college-bred peers of the media staffs, especially perhaps the millennial generation, processed through the universities at the present flood tide of postmodernism, lunged at the media bait, swallowing the hook, the sinker, and half of the line. They were not alone. Black Americans, already committed to salvation through Democratic politics, received the message that the Republican Party had nominated an outright racist. Women, overwhelmingly younger women, but many others, received the message that the Republican Party had nominated a misogynist insensitive toward the "weak" (handicapped). Hispanics received the message that the Republican Party had nominated an anti-Hispanic authoritarian.

Much of the Republican leadership cracked under the media pressure. House Majority Leader Paul Ryan disavowed his party's Presidential candidate based on the Mexican judge story and the "pussy tape." At the second Presidential debate, by the way, as soon as the "pussy tape" was introduced, Mr. Trump simply apologized, saying he was not proud of it, it was inappropriate, and it did not represent who he was now, over a decade later. The media instantly rejected this apology, on behalf of all American womanhood, as insincere and inadequate, and went full speed ahead in their caricaturing of Mr. Trump.

For the media, there was only one unforeseen problem—but it was one that on election eve and after had them confused, flushed with embarrassment, and, if only momentarily, humble. "Where did we go wrong?" "How did we get it so wrong?"

The variants on those themes have been multitudinous and they continue today, in the wake of what is called the "greatest election upset" in history. How did the polls (with exceptions I mentioned), the press analysts, and the pundits almost uniformly declare that candidate Trump did NOT represent *any* common American values and would be resoundingly repudiated in the election? "How did we get it so wrong?"

Election Eve 2016

On election eve, the TV anchors and panelists awaited the Clinton victory—yes, there was nervousness--only two days earlier, the FBI had concluded, abruptly, that it had no recommended charges based on its new investigation of Secretary of State Clinton's possible criminal abuse of classified intelligence information. A bit of a cliffhanger, but the polls reliably showed that in two days she had sprung back to leadership; all would be well.

They had fashioned, out of postmodernism's premises, a narrative of the politically correct first female candidate for President, bringing us together, and her opponent, the billionaire racist, misogynist, xenophobic, cripple-teasing bigot and "divider." And they had believed this story themselves, as we believe, however improbably, what confirms our deepest assumptions, and focused on the part of their audience who also believed them. And never imagined that any serious, significant remnant of Americans would fail to accept their fable.

Indeed, election eve began, as had the election, with New York, California, Illinois, and "Bosnywash" (the Boston to New York to Washington metropolitan corridor) unassailably in the Democratic camp with well over a hundred electoral votes for Hillary Clinton. On election eve, she never got above 215. The other bastion supposedly was Florida, where the great Miami-Dade-Broward County urban area went overwhelmingly for Clinton, but the rest of the state narrowly offset this to give Trump a pivotal victory.

On election eve, the panelists (as mentioned, I was following PBS Channel 13) watched anxious, then bewildered, then alarmed, then confounded as a brilliant red fire burned across America through state after state, region after region, where voters did not hear the postmodernist sirens screaming their alarm at "Miss Piggy" or the women who came out the past to charge "inappropriate touching."

In one of the most indefatigable campaign schedules in history, a 70-year-old supposed "playboy" had made five campaign stops a day with high-energy, ringing appeals to "Make America Great Again." The spacious sweep of America between the two coasts heard a message that an America they increasingly could not understand, with ideals unrelated to their lives, would not in the end supplant the America they knew and loved.

As the drumbeat of postmodernist alarms threatened to drown out any opposition, Mr. Trump was drawing astonishing crowds to rally after rally. In the closing days and hours, Mr. Trump campaigned for the most part alone—the media said "lonely," "isolated," "rejected," "abandoned by his party"—but his supporters watched Hillary campaigning with entertainers like Jay-Z—who supposedly represented Black Americans—rapping about "ni**ers," "pimps," and "motherfu**ers" while the media rolled on about Mr. Trump's vulgarity and insensitivity. (Unbelievably, Mr. Trump heard about this and said, quite casually, to an audience, "I like Jay-Z.") It was vintage Trump: say what you believe and damn the torpedoes.

And so, the wild red fire blazed through the evening—Florida for Trump, North Carolina for Trump, Pennsylvania for Trump, Ohio for Trump, Iowa for Trump: All the supposed "battleground states," which Trump had to sweep, fell one by one. Reliable stones in the "blue firewall" that guaranteed Clinton's victory—such as Michigan and Wisconsin—fell to Trump.

I was watching the panelists literally begin to mumble, heads down, "So what went wrong...?" "We have to ask ourselves..." "Why didn't we see this coming?"

They had fashioned, out of postmodernism's premises, a narrative of the politically correct first female candidate for President, bringing us together, and her opponent, the billionaire racist, misogynist, xenophobic, cripple-teasing bigot and "divider." And they had believed this story themselves, as we believe, however improbably, what confirms our deepest assumptions, and focused on the part of their audience who also believed them. And never imagined that any serious, significant remnant of Americans would fail to accept their fable.

In brief, voters for Mr. Trump had heard his positions, almost obliterated in mainstream media coverage, and heard Clinton's "let us unite, stronger together," but had said, "No, we will not unite around the postmodernist slogans and goals. We will unite around, and vote for, OUR values."

Understanding the Vote

And now, we must bow briefly to a seemingly different group, namely those among the supposed postmodernist audience whose votes added to the consternation of the media. On November 8, some 8 percent of Black Americans, one-third of Hispanic Americans, and more than half of white women voted for Donald Trump to be their President. In assuming that politics is all about identity groups, that ideas are a function of oppressed and oppressor conflicts, the media simply missed millions of individuals they had taken for granted. One out of three Hispanic Americans saw reason in Mr. Trump's positions; one in twelve Black American perhaps—I am speculating—did not like being represented in the great struggle for America's values and future by Jay-Z and Beyoncé or perhaps agreed with Mr. Trump that Black-on-Black crime, not the police, are devastating our inner-cities; and more than half of white women voted on issues they saw as more important than the "pussy tapes" and "Miss Piggy." Who would ever have suspected?

A final factor, much speculated on, but impossible to quantify, are secret Trump voters. In our time, the only deadly sin we recognize—the only trespass warranting anathema–is being politically incorrect toward an "oppressed" group. This includes not only outright bigotry but any failure of "sensitivity." On virtually the first day of the campaign, after Mr. Trump's comment that Mexican criminals were being ejected across the border along with the millions of what he called "good people," it became profoundly suspect, at least in the New York I know, to withhold condemnation of Mr. Trump. After the Mexican-American judge saga, the "pussy tape" saga, the Miss Piggy saga, and the Kovaleski saga, admitting openness to the Trump message became like being, well, being a black man in

Mississippi in 1920 suspected of lusting for white women. It simply was not possible to socialize after committing the Trump heresy. Earlier in the campaign, my wife of some 20 years, told me: "I don't know if I could live with someone who voted for Trump."

Postmodern journalism staged managed this situation— consciously, I believe—because it reflects their own philosophical assumptions. Theirs is advocacy journalism, not reporting, and the advocacy was: stop Trump. Yesterday, I walked into a restaurant and spied a man, a lawyer living in Sag Harbor, with whom I had spoken at the very beginning of the campaign. He waved and said, "So … what did you make of all this?"

My habitual response to that inquiry, throughout the campaign, had been a pained smile suitable to any interpretation. He hesitated for a few seconds, watching me, then asked: "Did you vote for him?" He hastened to add, "I mean, I didn't want to ask before …" "No, no, of course not," I said.

He shrugged and rolled up his eyes. "Hey, I did. I voted for him. Couldn't stand more of the same." "Yeah,

I did, too," I said.

He replied "It's okay. It's over. Sit down, why don't you? Did you see this table in the *Post* of who voted for him? Amazing!"

Just two white, male, college-educated oppressors letting down their hair. He said, "You know, my whole practice is in immigration cases…"

If you manufacture a story, believe in it, and pay attention only to that part of your audience that also believes in it, you have no reason to be startled when reality contradicts you. That is what happened on election evening 2016. Still, we should credit the *New York Times* for letting their "public editor," Liz Spayd, assigned to represent reader views, to write on the day after election that *Times* stories in weeks leading up to the election portrayed "… a juggernaut of blue state invincibility that mostly dismissed the likelihood of a Trump White House."

The consequences are more serious than the cold-water bath that perhaps briefly awakened the postmodernist press. The frightening story they spun was taken seriously by much of their audience, by those attuned to the postmodernist message. This was no mind-game, no competition for ratings—that which preoccupied the media and was exploited to the hilt by Clinton and her operatives.

The Losers Act Out

An audience of educated, sensitive, attentive American men and women, and their children, became panicked as the election unfolded. Women told me they were taking anti-anxiety medications. Some mourned that they could not afford to leave the country. The media must have on its conscience families who so frightened their own children with the postmodernist narrative that, in the wake of the election, we see photographs of weeping, depressed Yale University undergraduate women.

After the briefest pause for shock at the election outcome, young men and women in the cities—first, New York City, Los Angeles, and San Francisco, but also elsewhere—are surging through the streets, lighting fires, snarling traffic, and getting arrested. The press shakes its collective head, mournfully, and says: "Look at these young people distressed by the election." President Obama, as always with reason and calm, urges restraint and even, in a post-meeting press conference, called Trump "a good guy."

The media and politicians have done their thing. The election is over. They are prepared to move on. Great game, everyone. See you in four years.

But not others, now radically polarized not by Mr. Trump but the postmodernist press and a ruthless and cynical Democratic candidate, working in synergy, who may have given us four years of confusion and division over America's leadership.

We end where we began, with postmodernism and its premises, particularly that all politics is, and must be, a zero-sum game played by oppressors and the oppressed. That appears to be the view of demonstrators carrying signs that read "Not our President." Police report that in New York City, at least, the majority of the demonstrators are under 16 years of age. Our kids took the media seriously; hey, it's all they know.

That much of American journalism staged a morality play about what was at stake in the 2016 Presidential election, tells us nothing about what to expect from President-Elect Donald Trump. Scant attention was paid to Mr. Trump's policy proposals, principles of government, and views of history. How many voters can state two or three of Mr. Trump's positions, except "the wall," halting and reversing illegal entry into America, and renegotiating some trade pacts?

The media demanded endless clarifications on "groping," but I would have wished to know if Mr. Trump had heard of John Locke's theory of property rights as indispensable to liberty—and what Mr. Trump thought of that, today. I would have wished to know how he understood the rash of mass murders in our schools—and the role of guns. I would have enjoyed a debate question on the proposition "that government is best that governs least." I would have asked what role government can hope to play in "Making America Great Again" in a nation made great by capitalism, voluntary action, and private philanthropy—the system that exists in its purist form when government is strictly limited in its functions and attends to the rule of law, not engineering "equality" or "greatness."

I would have foregone meeting the undeniably beautiful Alicia Machado to know the mind of the man who now will be President. He remains to me too much an enigma; I have hopes, but not much more.

Published November 22, 2016, in *The Savvy Street*.

Chapter 13

Truth and Honor on the Potomac

This week (Dec 27), I watched the "Kennedy Center Honors" special on television. The Center is the apex of glory for American performing artists, the political and cultural elite's nationalist celebration of their conception of America's "best."

The evening's celebration of legend James Taylor, who over decades of his life overcame all odds to manifest his genius, had a special meaning to me, in a small way, because as a cub reporter for the *Worcester Telegram*, about 1969, I was assigned late one afternoon to cover a live James Taylor concert that evening in nearby Framingham. It seems our entertainment star reporter, Jack Tubert, was otherwise engaged.

The significant federal government capital support for the John F. Kennedy Memorial Center for the Performing Arts (though it is required to raised private funds for programming and earns much of its keep), which is billed as the "national center for the performing arts"—a "nationalist" concept—merits another article.

Watching the "Honors," I saw President Barrack Obama and First Lady Michelle Obama in the audience. At first, Mr. Obama was bobbing his head in time with the music, dignified as always, then, singing along with Michelle, and, at last, up and dancing. Washington, the media, our "opinion makers" and supposed standard setters were united in the brilliance of the occasion.

The man who on January 20, 2017, will be inaugurated President of the United States was attacked during the election campaign, to an extent without precedent in U.S. electoral history, for a private comment made a decade earlier that seemed to speak of women as mere objects of sexual lust. And, for a comment, now proved misleading if not outright false, that "fat shamed" a "Miss Universe" contest winner. And these attacks went on throughout the campaign, focusing on these incidents dug up by the Clinton campaign well in advance, headlined by the press, and deplored thousands of times in TV talk shows. This coverage came to dominate the election almost to the exclusion of discussion of substantive issues. The issue of "character," we were told, trumps all. Mr. Trump's attitude toward women simply wasn't presidential. If he was elected, women of character might be driven by sheer distaste to expatriate.

Well, the "sexual predator"—a term applied to Mr. Trump—whose words supposedly alarmed our young daughters (a *New York Times* story)—although the "frightening material" was made ubiquitous by the *Times* itself—will be inaugurated President of the United States in January. President and Mrs. Obama will hold their noses, the actors and singers honored by the Kennedy Center will boycott the celebration, and the media will promote, analyze, and then express a national shame.

John F. Kennedy and "National Shame"

For the posture of upholding standards of decency and sexual propriety, it is unfortunate that the presidency of John F. Kennedy, now over half a century in the past, has been so thoroughly explored and documented by historians. One of the best is the dean of British historians, Paul Johnson, whose *A History of the American People* (New York City: HarperCollins, 1997), brings together what is known about Kennedy with balance and extensive documentation. Following is a sketch, with a few links to books on certain topics. For those interested in delving deeper, I recommend Johnson's peerless narration of U.S. history.

John F. ("Jack") Kennedy was made president by his father, Joseph P. Kennedy ("Old Joe"), a successful Boston businessman who almost certainly was a major bootlegger, an associate of crime families, and a ruthless political manipulator. He paid a team of writers to write or rewrite the Kennedy 'bestsellers': *While England Slept*, and later, *Profiles in Courage*, and, in both cases, had his henchman buy hundreds of thousands of copies to score a "bestseller." This is one small detail, of course, a fine stroke, but it illustrates how he operated throughout in using fraud and manipulation to advance Jack Kennedy's career. During Jack Kennedy's successive elections to the House, Senate, and the presidency, he purchased opposing Boston newspapers and bribed hundreds of church pastors to deal with the Kennedy "Catholic" problem. Kennedy's vice president, Lyndon B. Johnson, later commented that Kennedy was the most do-nothing senator he had ever encountered in his decades in Congress.

When John F. Kennedy ran for president in 1960 against then vice president Richard M. Nixon, Old Joe Kennedy stole the election for his son. At the time, this was a widespread allegation, though disputed, but now is history. In Chicago and Texas, the historically unprecedented close election went by a few thousand votes for Kennedy. We now know that the infamous Chicago Mayor Daley's machine, delegated crime family boss Sam Giancana, among many others, to fix the election. (Later, Kennedy shared a mistress with Giancana.) In Texas, Kennedy vice presidential candidate, Lyndon Baines Johnson, stole the vote in several corrupt Texas districts. The two crimes changed the outcome of an American presidential election. Today, this is a matter of record.

The philosopher and political commentator, Ayn Rand, later excoriated candidate Nixon for not challenging the stolen election and commented that his moral cowardice in not doing so cost America its tragic involvement in Vietnam because Nixon, like the president under whom he served, Dwight D. Eisenhower, was on record and committed in principle to opposing a ground war in Southeast Asia—maintaining that the war against communism was on the European front.

Kennedy is known, today, to have been addicted to promiscuous sex, grabbing any woman at hand, a pattern well-known to his staff and the press, but loyalty concealed—until Kennedy was gone. The press adored Kennedy, but despised Nixon for his record of anti-communism.

It was Old Joe who selected Jacqueline Kennedy to marry Jack for "class"; required Jack to marry her; and made a huge financial settlement to induce her to agree. Later, when she threatened to storm out of the marriage over Jack's infidelities, Old Joe greatly supplemented the financial package.

Kennedy insisted, we now know, that he needed some new sexual experience every day. Before each of the three famous presidential debates, Kennedy staff paid prostitutes to service Kennedy. On inauguration day, it is reported, Kennedy put his wife, Jackie, to bed in the White House, and then had a liaison with a prostitute. He secured sexual trophies from Hollywood, including Marilyn Monroe, later turned over to his brother Bobby, and covered up the traces of their involvement when she committed suicide.

This was the 1960's "sexual revolution" in full flower and I wonder how many in the audience at the Kennedy Center would reject that cultural watershed. Its philosophy was that sexual relations had no significance beyond pleasure, preferably drug-enhanced, much like a new guitar tune, or dope hit, or a rich dessert. President Kennedy was an exemplar of the 'Sixties, including the sexual revolution, and accepted and celebrated it as such—although the story naturally was kept from the unenlightened public. President William Clinton, product of the Sixties generation, used the most powerful political office in the world to seduce a 22-year-old White House intern into performing oral sex.

Do you bloody understand? It meant NOTHING! Stimulation, discharge, dismissal. A bodily function.

Candidate Trump insisted that his campaign for President include his wife, his grown children, and their spouses—all with serious responsibilities in the Trump businesses. But this was viewed by the media and cultural "elite" as hypocrisy. As Melania Trump was battered by the media, it seemed her sin was to be not only glamorous, but admiring of her husband and committed to her children. So very un-Sixties ...

Kennedy often had his daily sex fix in the White House marriage bed when Jackie was absent. At other times, in New York City, he used secret tunnels under the Carlyle Hotel to keep secret his liaisons with prostitutes procured by the Secret Service.

As I now watch the "Kennedy Center Honors" come to its climax, I see the Center's director thanking the audience and donors of the Center and recalling Kennedy's "commitment to idealism and a just America," following "our vision wherever it leads."

And now, a "Camelot" song is rising ... The voice soaring, the handsome young Kennedy on the screen behind.

"The dream ... the dream ..."

President Obama's face is caught by the camera with what seems an almost unbearable sense of history's burden of idealism.

But, over it all, especially the intensity of this last "Kennedy Honors" of the Obama administration, there is a sadness (Did you hear? Michelle Obama has "lost hope") at what is to come. How to endure that we will have a President who joked, in private, on the stage set of a daytime TV romance, about "groping ...?" Where will be honor? Uplift? Idealism?

The doubts are too grim to contemplate during this dazzling tribute to the American "Camelot" of John and Jacqueline Kennedy that are the Kennedy Center Honors.

Published December 31, 2016, in *The Savvy Street*.

Chapter 14

Not Another Peep, Streep!

It is difficult to conclude that Meryl Streep was mistaken in her grandstanding attack on President-Elect Donald Trump. Why? If she was "mistaken" that means she honestly thought she was speaking the truth. But the falsehood she repeated—with the "heart-felt," self-righteous sincerity she brought to her acting roles—has been exposed so often, and the truth is so easily available, especially to one with her connections and resources, that "mistaken" doesn't seem possible. "Lying" does.

And yet, I don't think that is what we must conclude. Because all day today, U.S. news media repeated the video clip of her remarks— literally dozens of times just on the one channel I watched—and never, at least that I heard, corrected or questioned her. Perhaps some commentator, somewhere, did so.

In case you were camping in the Maine Woods for the past two days, here is the story. At the Golden Globes on Sunday evening, Meryl Streep received the Cecil B. DeMille lifetime achievement award. She took advantage of the moment—as Hollywood types do more and more these days—to purvey her politics, and, as it turns out, to reveal that her intellect, if not her acting ability, does seem to be "over-rated."

Without naming President-Elect Trump, she said that "…the person asking to sit in the most respected seat in our country imitated a disabled reporter. Someone he outranked in privilege, power, and the capacity to fight back. It kind of broke my heart when I saw it. I still can't get it out of my head because it wasn't in a movie. It was real life."

(No, Meryl, you have lost the ability to distinguish between a movie and real life. It did not happen in real life, only in the fictionized version created and endlessly promulgated by the media.)

She continued, "And this instinct to humiliate, when it's modeled by someone in the public platform, by someone powerful, it filters down into everybody's life, 'cause it kind of gives permission for other people to do the same thing."

I was not the writer who uncovered the truth about this tale. That honor belongs to others, who discovered and told the real story of the 'disabled reporter'. Here it is, in brief:

At a rally on November 21, 2015, Mr. Trump said that he recalled reading in the press that on the night of the 9/11 attacks, Arab-Americans were cheering the attack on roofs in New Jersey. He said he knew it was not "politically correct" to say so, but that is the report he read.

Major news outlets immediately denied there ever had been such a report. The *Washington Post* did a "fact check" just to confirm this. Nope, no story, said the *Post*; another Trump whopper.

And then, oh heaven! It turned out that the *Washington Post's own* story by Serge Kovaleski, on September 18, 2001, had said that, and that police had arrested some of the demonstrators. Oh my, and the *Post* had just done a "fact check" of *all* media and reported finding nothing.

Two Washington Post agents, finding Kovaleski now working at the *New York Times*, pressed him and he backtracked on his story, saying, at least as quoted: "I certainly do not remember anyone saying that thousands or even hundreds of people were celebrating. That was not the case…as best as I can remember …"

True, Mr. Trump did say "thousands" and that was not confirmed (on September 16, 2001, news video merely said "swarms"). But this had nothing to do with the media smear campaign that followed. That campaign did not dwell on the numbers, but veered from the "New Jersey" story to a fabricated libel of Trump as mocking a disabled individual. Back to "identity politics." This is how it happened.

Confronted with this seeming recantation of the *Post* story, at a rally in South Carolina, Mr. Trump recounted the above explanation and, in one of his unrestrained moments, pantomimed the flustered reporter protesting "No, no, no—I never said that." Mr. Trump brushed his hands up and down, laughing at the reporter desperately denying the charge of having written a story published under his by-line 16 years ago and never doubted to this moment. And, just for good measure, he made a quite funny face of the horrified reporter.

It so happens that Mr. Kovaleski has a disability, one hand sometimes frozen in a curled-over position. Some enterprising photographer took a single frozen frame from the entire video of Mr. Trump's antics, at the precise moment his hand seemed to be curled down; the photographer then set this beside a photograph of the reporter, standing in the same pose as Mr. Trump, his hand curled down. There you go, a headline story: Trump mocks the disability of reporter. It was shown thousands of times with new captions like "What will we tell our children?"

But it achieved its goal: diverting attention from the *Washington Post*'s ridiculous "fact finding" report, missing its own story, and from Mr. Trump's point about Arab-Americans in New Jersey cheering the attack on the World Trade Center. For good measure, it added to his resume of outrages against identity politics that he mocked the disabled

The true account has been told, and the falsehood discredited, many times—although not in the "mainstream"—Liberal/Leftist—media. So perhaps we cannot conclude that Meryl Streep is a liar. Only a dupe of the media to which she gives credence because it squares with her own ideology. But, hours after the Streep revival of the story, the *Post* published another piece insisting that Donald Trump mocked a disability.

It is not true, as endlessly repeated, that the Democratic Party was the "big loser" in the 2016 Presidential election. After all, they had held the White House for eight years, Hillary Clinton won the popular if not the electoral vote, the U.S. media overwhelmingly accepted and promulgated the message of the Democratic candidate, and an anger, bitterness, and fear surrounds the coming inauguration of President-Elect Trump.

No, it was not the Democratic Party but the U.S. media that was a decisive loser. Liberal/Leftist newspapers like the *New York Times* and *Washington Post*, prestigious magazines from the *Atlantic* to the *Economist*, and most television channels apart from Fox News, pulled out all stops to defeat Donald Trump and (when their favorite, Senator Bernard Sanders, had lost the Democratic nomination) to elect Hillary Clinton president.

Supposed "news" pages and editorial pages, purported "news" reports and panel discussions, all dissolved into a virtually seamless propaganda campaign with the single goal of defeating Trump. Objectivity, neutrality, balance, and professional reporting—and then honesty, fairness, and perspective—were flung aside in the headlong and later panicked crusade to make the election come out the "right way." Convinced that they had succeeded, that the election would sweep Clinton into office and the press would be viewed as the nation's savior, the mainstream media awaited vindication, triumph, and gleeful selfcongratulation as election evening began.

But, at first tentatively, then with emerging conviction, and finally with stunning decision in states not even considered "in play" for Trump, the American electorate—outside the great urban areas identified with Democratic politics—rendered a clear verdict on the media's influence on their perception of American reality.

Don't expect the media to forgive this humiliation. The campaign against Trump has continued without interruption. The reporters, editors, pundits, and commentators hope to discredit and then destroy President Trump—as they earlier destroyed President Richard Nixon for his landslide defeat of another Liberal/Leftist darling, George McGovern, in 1972.

In this coming battle, the embarrassing public display by Meryl Streep, and its limitless exploitation by the media, is but an initial skirmish.

You are too beautiful for the sacrificial altar, Meryl. Not another peep, Streep.

Published January 10, 2007, in *The Savvy Street*.

Chapter 15

Driving Trump from Office: The First Skirmish

What I call the "Not Our President Elite" (NOPE) believes that a frighteningly ignorant, bigoted, and distinctly inferior America—not the America of NOPE—elected Donald Trump. Defeated in the election, not only for President, but for control of Congress and statehouses nationwide, NOPE must save America by reversing the election.

NOPE is an increasingly coordinated movement of news media, left-leaning groups, and legions of ideologues of today's New ("Postmodernist") Left that is pursuing two strategies for clawing back political power after the 2016 election. These strategies do not emerge from a "conspiracy"; in fact, they are classic means of "destabilizing" governments when an election's losers refuse to accept the verdict.

The first is to *create a permanent sense of crisis* by histrionically portraying every initiative of the Trump administration as warranting nationwide resistance. By framing every action of the new administration as outraging law, American values, and mere decency—and constructing a media drama with "news" stories, features, columns, and editorials striking poses of shock—NOPE can radicalize moderate opponents of Trump—those who fail to grasp that the Great Satan sits in the White House. (Yes, the apocalyptic pitch of NOPE is reminiscent of the oratory of Iran's fanatic leaders. Look at *Time*'s cover, this week, on Steve Bannon, senior White House advisor).

The second strategy is *to call out, and then transmute into alarming headline reports—and glamorize—street protests at every new "crisis,"* "outrage," and "threat to America." When thousands routinely take to the streets, called forth by media outlets and "activist" groups, the quality of political discourse plunges. More participants take to the streets because they are assured that another outrage is occurring. All our experience suggests that young people in street demonstrations are aroused to a sense of revolutionary urgency, defiance of an outrage, and, above all, being "in"—belonging to the right side. Incited repeatedly, they become the mobs of the kind that third-world politicians mobilize at will.

Why Not Argue?

Almost immediately after the November 8 election, violence by college and even younger students filled TV screens. Speakers notable for their opposition to Postmodernism no longer could speak on campuses; the administration could not "guarantee their safety." What is notable on campuses is the absence of *argument.* If speaker Charles Murray or Ann Coulter has a viewpoint offensive to students, why not boycott the speech, why not invite opposing speakers? Or sponsor discussions of the ideas with faculty members who disagree with the speakers? Why not write and publish exposes of the speakers and their views? Why not *argue*?

Here is the most revealing manifestation of Postmodernism. Enlightenment philosophers identified reason as man's only means of discovering truth; in disagreements, they appealed to objective reality, to the facts. Challenging Modernism, the German Idealists, above all, perhaps, Friedrich Nietzsche, emphasized that each individual creates his own truth, by *will.* The *Ubermensch*, or ideal superior man, creates his own values by his will. That is the philosophical tradition of Postmodernism that shaped the ideas of Sartre and Foucault. A prime logical implication is that *your* truth is absolute; my truth is absolute. And if we clash? There is no common reference point, no objective reality, no arbiter of our argument. What is left is the response of students to ideas that offend their feelings, but with which they are unable to argue: violence. And so, the response to viewpoints no longer politically correct on campus is a riot. You will understand if I say I do not view the rioters as Nietzschean "supermen" but kids betrayed by the faculties paid to educate them.

Trump's Immigration Order

Just a week into the new Trump administration, protestors were called out to protest at airports around the country against the administration's order to review U.S. immigration security. The day that Trump authorized the review, the *New York Daily News* ran a one-word headline, filling its front page: "Crisis." News outlets in the reliable political hotspots—New York City, Washington, Chicago, Los Angeles— rang the tocsins of alarm. By Sunday, the protestors were at a few airports, especially JFK in New York, chanting, shouting, and waving signs, including the old standby of the Left: "No Fascist USA."

My crucial premise here is that the administration's initiative is decidedly moderate. Throughout his campaign, Trump promised that he would temporarily halt immigration from countries breeding radical Islamic movements, such as I.S.I.S, until he could be sure that the "vetting" process was identifying and barring terrorists. The seven countries chosen as presenting an active threat were listed in fact by the outgoing Congress and the Obama administration.

He mandated a pause in entry into the United States by refugees from Iran, Iraq, Syria, Libya, Somalia, Sudan, and Yemen. You may recognize that these countries have been in the news continuously in reports on terrorism, including military progress and devastation by ISIS. Refugees from the seven are barred from entering the United States only for 90 days. There is an indefinite ban on admitting more of the millions of refugees from Syria, an ISIS stronghold. Trump pledged in his campaign to reduce risk while reviewing how people entering the United States from those countries are screened to identify threats. After the review, entry into the United States opens, again, with whatever additional vetting might be added.

Problems, Yes, But A *Crisis*?

One can argue with the program. There are vetting procedures set up by the Obama and previous administrations. The seven nations have majority Muslim populations and thus, although entry is barred without regard for religion, the United States is singling out Islamic nations. There must be a rumor that terrorists seem to be of that faith. In fact, however, most countries with large Muslim populations are *not* included in the program. Coming from another point of view, the program could be attacked as cynically limited. Saudi Arabia, one of the world's sources of funds for terrorist organizations, is not included. Nor is Egypt, whose refugees in Europe have been implicated in attacks on women, including gang rapes of teenaged girls. Why are these countries excluded? Probably because they are trading partners and political allies of the United States.

Notice that the program is so limited and moderate in its goals—a review of procedures—that media outlets quickly re-focused on the reallife "victims." An estimated 100 to 200 people already traveling when the order was signed reached U.S. airports and were detained. They had approved documents for entry, but the Trump executive order put on hold their entry.

To travel far, leaving a country in chaos, and arrive at the United States, weary but excited at the prospect of a new life in freedom—and then to be stopped and told there is a "problem"—must be disheartening. The news media swooped down on a few individuals in very "human" interviews. Lawyers rushed to court and obtained an order that travelers with valid papers could not be sent back. Headlines screamed that a court had blocked Trump. The crisis had reached a thrilling climax. A man from Iraq who had served U.S. troops there as an interpreter wept for the cameras, saying he had his papers and deserved to enter.

But even by the time the court issued the injunction, about 40 detainees, including the man from Iraq, *already* had been vetted and admitted to the country. The Trump administration's first initiative (apart from internal government reorganization), was not a "crisis," nor a "sweeping ban," nor an occasion for "Lady Liberty Weeps."

And yet, NOPE mobilized thousands of protestors. This may have been easier because it was the first call to protest after the new administration took office. Given reports of near illiteracy and ignorance of history and geography of many high-school and college students, I wonder if marching and chanting by torchlight may be more appealing than devising and expressing an argument. Earmarks of classic far leftist protests were apparent, including widespread use of "Fascist" to name any opponents.

As I reported during the election, the liberal-leftist press wagered everything on winning for their candidates (Sanders, then Clinton) and ideas. They jettisoned objectivity, factuality, and balance—and later flung aside fairness and even decency—in their headlong drive for victory. Despite their defeat, their campaign radicalized (not to mention, frightened) millions of Americans, perhaps especially women.

Humiliated, NOPE vowed permanent protest. There were repeated calls never to "normalize" Trump. NOPE's goal is to make it impossible for Trump to govern—and, better still, to drive him out of office. And they have in mind an inspiring precedent.

The Great Watergate Media Triumph

Ayn Rand observed the same pattern when Richard Nixon, in 1972, defeated the darling of left-liberalism, Sen. George McGovern, and the media began a crusade to regain its dignity. In an *Ayn Rand Letter* dated April 9, 1973, entitled "Brothers, You Asked for It!" she began with incomparable drama: "I had hoped to write a letter, someday, entitled 'Why I Will Not Write About Watergate'—and explain that "I do not take part in lynching."

Although Rand had endorsed Nixon in the 1972 election, she did not champion him in Watergate, except to say that this was a *lynching*, given the actual "crimes" alleged, and that Nixon's philosophical pragmatism had delivered him to his enemies—enemies who also were pragmatists. But she highlighted the true origin of the lynch-mob loathing of the President, writing that "A touch of gloating hatred for the political Right breaks through ... in the form of an attempt to involve half-a-nation (or more) in their [liberal-left media] broad ideological smear." The "half a nation (or more)" were those who defied the press by defeating McGovern and giving Nixon a historical landslide victory. Probably many younger Americans who bought into the rationalizations for a campaign of vindictive character assassination never knew that Nixon's unforgiveable "crime," as Paul Johnson traces in his history referenced below, was lifelong anti-communism.

The media hailed themselves as heroes for "saving the nation" by staging Watergate; the public bought the story. People still believe in the "Watergate" legend. But historians have had time to review the record. The dean of British historians, Paul Johnson, in *A History of the American People* (New York City, 1997), reviewing the events, concludes that "...the anti-Nixon campaign, especially in the *Washington Post* and the *New York Times*, was continual, venomous, unscrupulous, inventive, and sometimes unlawful.... [T]he hysteria usually associated with American witch-hunts took over and all reason, balance, and consideration for the national interest was abandoned (pp. 901-3)." That will sound familiar if you were awake during the 2016 election.

The media will try to reenact their Watergate victory with President Trump. Trump cannot stop them from trying, but he can deflate their credibility with well-planned initiatives—some commendably radical, like cutting the EPA down to size—implemented in a way that minimizes "collateral damage"—like passengers stuck in airports. He can minimize his off-handed comments that are so easy to seize upon out of context; my own initial impression is that he is doing so.

President Trump must continue his confrontation of the media and his other critics. He must not hope to call a ceasefire with his enemies. Such a ceasefire will be observed on only one side. But his frank reprimands of the media must be factually correct and impeccably logical. His rebukes must be found to be accurate when his enemies and supporters finish investigating.

Meanwhile, get used to Watergate reruns.

Published February 23, 2017, in *The Savvy Street.*

Chapter 16

Going Nowhere: Utopia in An Age of Politics

I am feeling my age. Make that "Age."

I feel as though since the Republican National Convention in July 2016, I have done nothing but think, talk, write, post, and everything but pray (and that may be coming) about politics. So far, I have not taken to the streets—bad company. Although for much of my life, since I read *Atlas Shrugged* at age 17, 55 years ago, I have been active in politics in an intellectual sense, and always concerned, the past few months feel like a climax.

I supported Donald Trump; others did not. But I observe around me people viewing our day as apocalyptic (or is it just that I still check the front page of the *New York Times*)? This evening's blow-out about the exclusion of three reporters from a White House briefing is typical. I'm with President Obama: "It isn't the end of the world until the world ends." What we are witnessing is but one new episode in one long, all-encompassing drama. The drama is the Age of Politics.

Through the Ages

Reading about the Age of Faith, Age of Enlightenment, and Age of Science—all eras in the history of the West—did you ever ask: what is *our* age? There have been bids to name it, of course: the age of anxiety, the age of technology, the space age, and the information age.

All of them have a claim, but how would you go about choosing one? I suggest this test: In any given extended period of history—say, at least a century, usually longer—what did mankind view, explicitly and implicitly, as the *key to salvation,* or human destiny, or being human? What did people take for granted as "where the action is" in attaining man's highest potential?

I feel a certain sadness when I make the obvious point that not every age was an Age of Politics likes yours and mine. There was the "Age of Faith," also called the Middle Ages (550 A.D. to 1350 A.D.), when the dominant influence in Western civilization was the Church of Rome (although during this period outside the West, Islam arose and asserted itself). In these centuries, the salvation of the human soul was all about faith in God and faith was manifested in literature, music, architecture, and the very structure of philosophy. More down to earth, it was an age when the workforce clearing the seemingly limitless forests of Europe for agriculture was the huge monastic movement.

Yes, political battles occurred everywhere, but were usually fought in terms of religion; the great wars were wars of religion. Arguably, the Age of Faith was the most embracing of "totalitarianism"—invasion of every possible facet of life--in history until today's Age of Politics.

The Renaissance (1300 to 1700) is also called the Age of Humanism, or the Age of Man, celebrating in some of the world's greatest literature, painting, sculpture, and architecture the glory and centrality of human beings and human life on earth.

The Age of Science (1550 to 1800) –well, I will not elaborate on each age. I may devote future essays to different "ages" in Western civilization and how Ayn Rand in the 20th Century became a dominant philosophical inspiration for new generations of intellectuals to explore, understand, appreciate, and carry forward the greatness of the Western tradition from every age.

The Age of Enlightenment (1620 to 1800) —in some ways, the most intensely focused and glorious—saw the courageous questioning of religion and even faith, as such, reverence for scientific knowledge, and rejection of superstition and prejudice. The unafraid quest for knowledge in all areas of human life was to all educated persons the obvious human destiny, the human task on earth.

Although often identified with the Enlightenment, the Age of Reason (1701 to 1799), extended the Enlightenment ideal of knowledge and insight into religion, art, science, and other fields, but also focused intensely on organized, *systematic philosophies* to guide all human activities. All decisions facing mankind could be referred to the consistent light of reason and settled by logic. Perhaps the single most influential document urging American colonists to revolt against England was a mere pamphlet, "The Age of Reason," by Thomas Paine. At the extremes, as in the French Revolution, intellectuals applied their supposed rational consistency in all things to the guillotine and the desecration and looting of churches. If there seemed too much in the world of the actions of fanatical madmen, well, then the world was not yet guided by the pure light of right reason.

Other "ages" have been proposed, but these broad labels have become history's acknowledged chapter headings. One additional label, "The Age of Romanticism," describes a real, powerful, and glorious phenomenon throughout the Western world. Is it too narrow to characterize as an "age"? Or, as claimed by some, was it the "anti-Enlightenment, the transition from the Age of Reason to something much worse—Postmodernism?"

I will take that up another day.

Ours Is the "Age of Politics"

The Age of Politics: Did it start with the publication of *The Wealth of Nations* in 1776? Again. it becomes obvious that "ages" don't succeed one another like centuries. *The Wealth of Nations* was a product of the Age of Reason and established the political economy of capitalism in the West. It was socialism that challenged the ideas of Adam Smith and, indeed, the moral legitimacy of the Industrial Revolution and the dominance of capitalism. I would designate the year 1848, when the pamphlet *The Communist Manifesto* was published in Germany by Karl Marx and Friedrich Engels, as the start of the Age of Politics.

Politics, of course, did not come to dominate human thinking in a year or a decade. Its influence unfolded over time so that the peak of capitalism's *practical* success was in the 1880's and 1890's (the latter a decade of such obvious optimistic happiness as to warrant the historic label "the Gay Nineties"). But in the theoretical realm, the Age of Politics was gaining rapidly. The Progressive Movement in America challenged laissez-faire. In Europe, in 1918, the Bolsheviks seized power from the newly liberated democratic government of Russia and imposed the murderous communist government. Less than a decade later, the New Deal brand of socialism gained the presidency in the United States. At the same time,

National Socialism was rising in Germany with Hitler's ascent—while in Italy, fascism emerged.

These systems and variants were proposed as blueprints for salvation from devastating malaise; they were sold as human utopias and the buyers were idealist youth. So compelling was the destiny promised to mankind by these systems that their leaders soon accepted that any number of deaths, and enslavement of the living, could be justified as a transition to mankind's final, permanent happiness.

The 20th Century became a human nightmare with two world wars in rapid succession; totalitarian dictatorships murdering, starving, and enslaving country after country—Russia, Germany, Japan, China, the rest of Eastern Europe, Cuba, Southeast Asia … The resilient capitalist nations in Europe, North America, and parts of other continents, with strong traditions of freedom and the economic might of capitalism, did not succumb. They joined the Age of Politics, however, by means of decades of fevered attempts, gradually successful, to introduce socialism; in these nations, too, the decisive consideration for the future of mankind, the great struggle of the era, was political.

Not that other developments were absent; science and technology transformed first the West and then much of the world. Education, to an extent never known in history, became universal and higher education a mass movement. Computing and availability of information increased by huge orders of magnitude. Transportation in our era is so different from earlier eras as to be radically discontinuous with man's entire earlier history. With this impressive competition, a crucial premise in awarding the crown to an Age of Politics is that those other elements of life, though powerful, transformative, and even triumphant (e.g., technology) were not and are not viewed as the keys to our destiny, to the decisive human struggle, to salvation. That role is reserved for politics.

For much of the past century, we have asked: Will the world "go communist" and end all our hopes? For many hundreds of millions in many countries, this happened. Will America internally travel the familiar path to socialism—of the fascist variety of socialism, as Ayn Rand explained? Or will capitalism re-emerge, strong and fully consistent, and so save America and lead us at last to the "Utopia of Greed"—as Ayn Rand entitled the chapter in *Atlas Shrugged* introducing "Galt's Gulch"? In all ages, men viewed human happiness as at stake in the (designated) "decisive" question of their time—faith, enlightenment, science, reason. Perhaps, though, our age has the best justification for doing so. The Age of Politics saw the birth of totalitarianism in government: government's absolute dictation of every area of human life. If in earlier times, dictators and authoritarians had left little freedom in government or the practice of religion, other sectors of life remained comparatively open for those who conformed in areas under dictation. In the Age of Politics, not surprisingly, all of man's life—education, work, marriage, childrearing, art, science, travel, speaking and publishing, military service, any aspect of economic life—came within government's scope. To the extent that the Age of Politics meant living under freedom versus totalitarianism, then, indeed, politics was decisive.

An Age that Cannot Self-Correct

Among Ayn Rand's boons to philosophy was lucid identification of the hierarchy of knowledge, with fundamentals of metaphysics and epistemology underlying and implying theories of ethics, politics, and art. The agony of the Age of Politics is that its disputes, wars, and experiments with millions of individual lives never can be resolved on the level of politics. Politics is a branch of philosophy proceeding from metaphysics (our view of the nature of man), epistemology (our view of reason and the requirements of knowledge), and ethics (our view of the goals and standards of choice and action). Thus, disputes in politics cannot be resolved without reference to fundamental philosophy. No demonstration of the productivity of free markets, the failures of the command economy, or the misery of life under socialism will resolve the disagreements of the age of politics. Collectivism proceeds inescapably from the morality of altruism—the creed that sanctions the sacrifice of some individuals for the supposed good of others. Capitalism proceeds from the morality of egoism, the moral right of everyone to live for his own sake with his own values and happiness as the goal of his life.

As urgent as politics seems today—angst was fueled nonstop by the media during the election to scare voters away from the Republican candidate—our destiny does not lie in politics. If the human future is being decided, today, it is in the "culture wars" pitting Postmodernism against remnants of Enlightenment Modernism. In politics, Postmodernism has its incarnation in New Left views such as egalitarianism, permanent struggle of the "oppressed" against the "oppressors," humankind's subservience to the "natural order," and the undercutting of the standards of Western culture in the arts, literature, consumerism, and, of course, sex, marriage, and family.

I have risked high hopes on President Trump. If he keeps his promises on regulations, energy and the environment, the Supreme Court, taxes, law enforcement, vouchers for education, and assertion of American national self-interest abroad—and has no truck with Postmodernism's political correctness—then, at least in politics and government American decline might slow.

But if you would "Make America great again"—a slogan that implies the *false* premise that politics is the key to human success—then give your mind, effort, and hope to a new age in philosophy.

Published March 31, 2017, in *The Savvy Street*.

Chapter 17

Social Media Freedom in the Crosshairs

This week, the "old" news media (I prefer "old" to "mainstream" and certainly to "professional") showed further signs of zeroing-in on a scapegoat for their devastating defeat and humiliation in the 2016 election. The scapegoat is the "social media."

We saw it coming. But this weekend, the first story in the *New York Times Magazine* was "Click Bait," designating President Donald Trump as "troll-in-chief" and launching into a sophisticated, extended smear reminiscent of the (also "old") Left—that he is a "fascist."

An Academic Report (with a Grant from Soros)

The same weekend, the Columbia School of Journalism released a report commissioned by George Soros's Open Society Foundation, entitled *Study: Breitbart-led Rightwing Ecosystem Altered Broader Media Agenda*. Can't make it clearer than that, right?

Oh, wait. I can run that through the Google translation system. Got it. "Upstart internet news organizations, abetted by millions on Facebook and Twitter, prevented the *New York Times* and *CNN* from defeating Trump." Thank you, Google. Clearer, now.

As an "academic" report, the Columbia analysis, of course, is "neutral." Beginning factually enough, the report says that in the wake of "an election that shook the foundations of American politics," the (old) media "looked for an external disruption to explain the unanticipated victory—with theories ranging from Russian hacking to "fake news."

This seems like a promising beginning. Then, the next paragraph established the report's thesis—and tone—and may hint at the line of attack the media is going to take. Here, the Columbia School of Journalism is admonishing its graduates in positions throughout the American "old" media to focus on the *real* problem—and target. The next paragraph names that target:

We have a less exotic, but perhaps more disconcerting explanation: Our own study of over 1.25 million stories published online between April 1, 2015 and Election Day shows that a rightwing media network anchored around Breitbart used social media as a backbone to transmit *a hyperpartisan perspective to the world.*

To understand what they mean by "hyper-partisan" do we contrast it with the coverage of the election by the *New York Times*, *Washington Post*, and *CNN*? There *is* no more "hyper-partisan" than their coverage of the election. I documented again and again their false charges, fake news, transparent slanting, and shameful double standard in relentlessly attacking Donald Trump. Even supporters of Trump may not grasp the extent of the blatant distortions.

But to return to that paragraph, we see the targets all in a row: "rightwing media network," "Breitbart," "social media," and "hyperpartisan perspective."

Of course, these diligent researchers did not read and analyze 1.25 million media stories. As they explain, there are software programs that analyze who "shares" online media stories–say by "tweeting" or "sharing" or "hyperlinking." How many stories from a given publication are shared? If a reader shares a story, what other publications does that reader follow and share? There are many daunting cluster charts and diagrams.

My conclusion is that the Breitbart organization ought to send a *big* check for publicity and advertising to the Columbia School of Journalism. The chart-and jargon-battered reader now knows that the Breitbart organization, and all the rightwing news sites it "anchors," managed to determine the outcome of the 2016 election in the world's most information- and communications-rich, educated, and politically powerful nation. Wow! What a prospectus for an initial public offering!

And when did this daring David stride onto the scene to challenge the world's largest, best-funded, and most—um– "professional" media? Breitbart began in 2007, less than a decade ago. The writers of the report did not (entirely) miss the irony. They write, and the paragraph is worth quoting:

A remarkable feature of the right-wing media ecosystem is how new it is. Out of all the outlets favored by Trump followers, only the *New York*

Post existed when Ronald Reagan was elected president in 1980. By the election of Bill Clinton in 1992, only the *Washington Times*, Rush Limbaugh, and arguably Sean Hannity had joined the fray. Alex Jones of Infowars started his first outlet on the radio in 1996. Fox News was not founded until 1996. Breitbart was founded in 2007, and most of the other major nodes in the right-wing media system were created even later.

I do hate to interrupt this tribute to the triumphant insurgence, in just a few decades, against the once almost unchallenged liberal-left agenda for an ever-growing interventionist-welfare state. But I am wondering, about here: Did this "right wing" media David step forth, seize the attention of an unsuspecting American electorate, and bring down the liberal-left establishment's Goliath in 2017? Or did Americans no longer willing to tolerate the leftward drift and arrogant dictation of politically correct opinion of the "old" media—apparent and metastasizing since at least the mid-1960's–provide the explosive impetus and audience that thrust the new media to prominence and joined it in the defeat of Hillary Clinton and the election of Donald Trump?

The report avoids denouncing any position taken by the political candidates. Nothing being judged right or wrong here, folks. It is just that the "right-wing" media is "hyper-partisan," "insulated," "extreme," and "propagandistic." Right-wing media skillfully blended bits of facts with "false and misleading narratives." Right-wing media "consistently attack" reporters in the old news media.

Or, to sum it up, as "neutrally" as is possible for them:

What we find in our data is a network of mutually-reinforcing hyper-partisan sites that revive what Richard Hofstadter called "the paranoid style in American politics," combining decontextualized truths, repeated falsehoods, and leaps of logic to create a fundamentally misleading view of the world.

But this report, as Mr. Soros intended, presents itself as nonpartisan. It emphasizes that it made no evaluation of the contents of the media outlets analyzed. It did not need to do so. That piece of the puzzle, for the alert reader tuned-in to the opinion-center of the Universe (New York City, where the Open Society Foundation, *New York Times*, and Columbia School of Journalism are located) quickly was supplied.

The New York Times Paints the Bull's Eye

The lead story in the *New York Times Magazine*, March 5, 2017, by Amanda Hess, and with the title "Click Bait," reached for an explanation in terms of *cortext* for the disaster suffered by the liberal-left and the "old" media:

Over the course of Donald Trump's staggering political rise, observers tried to make sense of him by borrowing a metaphor from the internet: Trump, they said, was a troll.

Let me interrupt, briefly, to say that, as an observer throughout the primary and elections, this explanation of Trump never occurred to me. What I noticed, first, was his rather consistent stand against burgeoning government power, a series of positions staked out against taxes, regulations, the attack on the energy industry in the name of "climate change," the public-education lobby against such innovations as vouchers, and proliferation of government power into the arts, humanities, and higher education.

A "smear" can be crude— "you're a fascist"—or it can be sophisticated, requiring two and half pages of the *New York Times Magazine*.

First, Ms. Hess, whose media reputation was made writing about "gender," especially that the internet is misogynist, threatening to women, first establishes that candidate Donald J. Trump is a "troll." She defines "troll" for us as "a figure that skips across the web, saying whatever it takes to rile up unsuspecting targets, relishing the chaos in his wake and feasting on attention, good or bad."

I hope that clarifies the nature of a "troll" as contrasted with the controversial poster of ideas and opinions who angers some readers, including "unsuspecting targets." As for "relishing the chaos" and "feasting on attention"—you'll have to let us know how you can tell, Ms. Hess.

I mean, do *you* post on Facebook or Linked-In or Twitter? If so, do you, skipping across the web," rile anyone? Are they "unsuspecting"? Do you "relish the chaos" and "feast on the attention"? Are you a troll?

Ms. Hess begins her article by quoting assertions that President Trump is a "troll." And ends, triumphantly, with quoting an anonymous internet user who called Trump "the most superior troll." Trump replied, rejecting the implied smear of equating his use of Twitter to reach tens of millions of voters with the vague negative connotation of "troll," by responding "a great compliment." I mean, the Columbia report says that the guy, not exactly of the "computer generation," mastered this medium well enough to defeat a phalanx of old media Goliaths to become President of the United States.

Having established Mr. Trump as a "troll," Ms. Hess now simply calls the roll of "trolls" whom she wishes to associate with (smear over) Mr. Trump. It is as transparent and dishonest as an article earnestly discussing Dopey, Sleepy, Sneezy, Doc, and Donway. Get it? All dwarfs!

Her tale, she says, is about "Troll culture as forged in the primordial ooze of the internet…" She begins with the apparently infamous troll "Mr. Bungle, a character dressed as a clown in a semen-stained costume." And, jumping to 2014, "the video game developer, Zoe Quinn, in an affair that became #gamergate." Apparently, Milo Yiannopolous, then social media reporter for *Brietbart News*, commented on that controversy. Are you following the links? So far, no mention of President Trump.

Finally, we make the connection. The chief executive officer of Breitbart, which hired Mr. Yiannoplous as a reporter, who wrote on "#gamegate," is Steven K. Bannon, who became Mr. Trump's election campaign advisor. Ms. Hess drops her troll chain-of-association, for now, and darts back to the French philosopher, Existentialist John-Paul Sartre, after World War II, writing about anti-Semites and that they were not "unaware of the absurdity" of their view. Now, Ms. Hess takes us back to the present, with, she promises, a "resurgence of this winking Nazi type…"

Do you see the long smear spreading? So far, Mr. Trump has owned to being a "troll" because he discovered that the social media, a direct daily connection with tens of millions of voters, circumvented the iron grip of the "old" media and its interpolation of his views to his audience. He could wake up in the morning, read a new headline attacking him, and not wait until his staff issued a press release that the media might pick up later in the day. He could reply instantly, taking the initiative away from the media for the first time in American history.

But now, somehow, we are talking about Jean-Paul Sartre and anti-Semites. It gets better. PewDiePie, apparently, is a game on YouTube that featured Nazi symbols. Okay, I believe you. From there, we skip without transition (none! Check it out!) to Richard Spencer, a proponent of white nationalism—the view that European civilization and its values are being diluted by cultures and races that will destroy its strengths. His followers cried "Hail, Trump!" at a rally.

Now, with no transition, we have a paragraph on David Duke, who showed up in Washington, says Ms. Hess, with a Pepe the Frog lapel pin (this seems to go back to the PewDiePie game) and was punched in the face while being interviewed.

Time to tie all this to the 45th president of the United States, who has triumphed over the combined power of the American corporate media, including by. .tweeting…and has refused to be smeared as a "troll."

Ms. Hess has only two paragraphs to go. I thought that I might summarize her final thoughts. I find myself unable to do so. How is she going to make a final dramatic swipe to spread the long, drawn-out smear over President Trump? I cannot find a way to generalize. Let Ms. Hess have her say:

Recently, we have witnessed a resurgence [from France before WWII] of this winking Nazi type. Pewdiepie, a wildly popular YouTube video game star, filmed a "prank" in which he hired two men to hold up a sign that said, "Death to Jews." Pepe the Frog, an online cartoon that morphed into 4chan meme, has been co-opted by plugged-in fascists who redraw him with swastikas as eyes. And after the white nationalist Richard Spencer…" and "These days even David Duke…is sharing racist memes and getting called a "troll."

Well, no mention of President Trump, yet, but the slingshot is drawn far back. In the final paragraph, Ms. Hess finally targets President Trump. She writes:

…Becoming President has blown Mr. Trump's cover: There's nothing more consequential than this. Trolls are typically outsiders, and sad ones. They don't fit into the dominant group, so they terrorize from the sidelines. Part of what makes the Trump administration so alarming is that the troll sensibility now dominates, And when that happens, it's reminiscent of what Sartre describes: "No reason, no principle, just pure exercise of power."

And there you have the smear. Mr. Trump a troll. Another troll is Mr. Bungle; Breitbart technology reporter, Yiannopolous, reports the Mr. Bungle story; Brietbart CEO, Steven Bannon, becomes advisor of Trump's campaign; Jean-Paul Sartre said anti-Semites are self-aware; a You-Tube game featured Nazi symbols; the followers of Richard Spencer, a white national, cry out "Hail Trump"; David Duke, associated with the KKK, shows up at a Washington meeting with a Pepe the Frog lapel pin; President Trump's "troll sensibility" dominates the White House.

Oh, go ahead, Ms. Hess! Just *say* that President Trump is a Nazi, an associate of Richard Spencer and David Duke, no doubt a fan of the Nazi YouTube game, and an anti-Semite.

Is yours, too, the "hate that dare not speak its name"?

But she can't do that because there is no logical connection. Not one. It is the nature of a smear to use guilt by association—though usually a little stronger than "association" by mere sequential mention in the same article. She has not quite mastered the smear.

Watch Your Back, "Social Media"

I discuss this article at length, more than its content deserves, because it is the kick-off piece in America's most reputable newsmagazine and it is a classic smear. By association with a list of internet trolls, and a flashback to Sartre, it smears the president of the United States as a Nazi.

In doing so, it completes the work of the report of the Columbia School of Journalism. That report, in the name of neutrality, did not mention the content—the ideas, the policies—upheld by the "rightwing" media. Ms. Hess's column supplies that content: Social media, as utilized by Mr. Trump, was a vehicle of anti-Semitic, Nazi propaganda.

The social media's CEOs are the target, here. They are gardenvariety liberals, eager to do the right thing, terrified to be distanced from the establishment—and now pushed to "patrol," "monitor," the content of what we write on Facebook and Twitter.

This would not be tolerated if it were a policy of the government toward the news media. But, rightly, "regulation" of activity on private speech platforms, like Facebook and Twitter, is entirely at the discretion of their owners.

It is too soon to tell if that is what the new enemies of "social media" are counting on. Certainly, social media CEO's have rushed to "cooperate." The "extremists" on the right have had their Twitter accounts closed. That has done little, so far, to silence the unruly outbreak on social media of opposition to the liberal-left.

We must await the next moves by enemies of the upstart social media: that is, by long-established news organizations fighting for their dominance of American public opinion. Just this week (March 7), it was reported that Facebook began to put "disputed" tags on fake news. If someone reports you, or a Facebook algorithm IDs you, your post is sent to two fact-checking organizations; if they both disagree with the post's statements, the post gets a "disputed" tag. These are small beginnings. As indicated by the two stories analyzed here, the crusade to swat down competition to the old media is just getting underway.

No viewpoint, opinion, argument is excluded ("filtered") from social media unless you become a target by achieving *too* much influence. The pure air of free thought, free exchange, is intoxicating.

It probably is too late to suppress the tens of millions of Americans who have experienced the satisfaction of expressing their views directly to others worldwide. Facebook and Twitter have toughened them to controversy, threats, insults, and sanctions such as "unfriending" and "blocking."

I can almost pity the grand old media. When I was growing up, our Republic, as represented by the "press," invited readers to send "letters to the editor." Get that? You have a disagreement with what we say? Another opinion? Only one place to send it for 'consideration": The editor. Wasn't that *enough* for you?

Now, the old media are up against freedom, and that can be painful. W.H. Auden wrote:

"We wandered lost on the mountains of our choice
And wept, freedom was so wild..."

Published March 24, 2017, in *The Savvy Street*.

[This chapter may strike readers as a long aside in the drama of Trump's electoral upset. From the start, Trump's enemies cast his candidacy in Postmodernist terms. New York Times *columnist Paul Krugman lamented that Trump's strength revealed that "white nationalism"—racism—was more widespread in America than we would have hoped. And so, from the outset, Trump was framed as the enemy of "multiculturalism." When Trump took on Steven Bannon, head of upstart online news organization* Breitbart News, *in August 2016, as his campaign CEO, the "white nationalist" charge went into orbit. Bannon appears to be a "nationalist," but not related to race. His conviction is that the shared language, culture, and traditions of Americans—however internally diverse—are the foundation of their political polity. And that foundation is now stressed to the breaking point by infusion of new languages, cultures, and therefore political ideals by illegal millions permitted by uncontrolled immigration.*

In this article, from a personal perspective, I "tried on" the framework of "cultural nationalism" or "civic nationalism" --and invited readers to do the same.]

Chapter 18

Is There a Rational Nationalism?

I haven't made up my mind about the debates regarding "nationalism," conducted mostly in terms of epithets and denials that have poisoned political debate since Donald Trump burst onto the U.S. political scene. "Nationalism" has been defined as an aspect of our selfidentification with our country or "homeland" that is "…based on shared characteristics such as culture, language, race, religion, political goals or a belief in a common ancestry." More narrowly, it has been defined as the favoring of self-government by those living in a nation" rather than by an occupying power, say, or a colonial power. Yet another definition, which takes us into the controversy that arose in the 2016 election, is "the policy or doctrine of asserting the interests of one's own nation viewed as separate from the interests of other nations or the common interests of all nations."

Our overnight-most-famous contemporary "nationalist" is Steven Bannon, the successful businessman, movie producer, and revolutionary media innovator who became the head of President Trump's successful election campaign and is now a national security advisor. That Mr. Bannon has become perhaps the most feared, loathed, and attacked (and smeared) man in America says little about his views, but everything about the god of American "progressivism": multiculturalism.

Multiculturalism is the contemporary brand name of "cultural relativism," the view that there cannot be an objective standard by which to judge the relative merits of different cultures. It is a variant of subjectivism, which argues that each of us, inescapably, sees the world from "inside" his culture (as well as his sex, economic class, race, and ethnicity) and that limits our ability to discern truth. Therefore, each culture must be accepted and judged strictly on its own terms.

It is worth mentioning, parenthetically, that "globalism," especially economic globalism, does not entail "multiculturalism"—only the view that under conditions of free trade, free movement by workers, and peace, every individual in every country potentially can benefit far more than under economic nationalism. Globalism does not refuse to apply objective moral standards to other countries; but rests on belief that a global free economy produces the greatest benefits for any group, including any cultural group, that participates.

Varieties of Nationalism

Mr. Bannon has been called, or labeled, a "white nationalist" over and over, daily, in what has become a kind media tic, a political Tourette's syndrome. He has denied it. What is interesting is that he is a selfproclaimed nationalist, a European cultural nationalist, who argues that cultural, social, and political values from the Western European tradition have shaped what is distinctive and essential about America and that America cannot survive as America if most of, or even many of, her citizens do not espouse these values.

Although this is anathema to the multiculturalists—implying that American culture is exceptional, must be preserved, and is in danger of "dilution" by other cultures—it is not their typical charge against Mr. Bannon. Their charge remains that he is a "white nationalist." Why? I believe because "white nationalism" is easily and rightly denounced as racism: discrimination based upon inherited biological characteristics— not on the choices that make up an individual's morality and character. "Cultural" nationalism is a philosophical concept dealing with ideas and values available to any individual. What is hateful about this to multiculturalists is that it valorizes a given culture (Western, European, and American) over others.

Of the many forms of "nationalism," including identification of a nation's essential character as racial, religious, or ethnic, the one favored by traditional (true) liberals has been "civic nationalism," the view that a nation is defined and sustained by a certain view of the role of government, the rights and responsibilities of citizens, and how government earns its legitimacy (e.g., democratic procedures). From what I have read of Mr. Bannon's views, he seems to believe that sustaining "civic nationalism" depends upon sustaining underlying ideas and values. Put thus generally, I can agree: philosophical premises underlie and undergird political principles. It is worth noting that Mr. Bannon specifically and vehemently rejects the "*Atlas Shrugged* sort of view," which he sees as unrelated to underlying American culture.

Because any culture comprises the philosophical ideas (including political premises), the moral values, traditions, sense of life, and common literature and other art of a majority in a country, Objectivism rejects cultural relativism, boldly asserting rational standards for comparing the relative merits of different cultures. In a nation where large minorities of people have different cultures—say, French and English culture in Canada or American and Latino in the United States—the same judgments can be made. Of course, assessments of a given culture tell us little about any individual. No one knows that better than Objectivists who know the tale of the Russian Jewish girl who gave her heart to French Romantic literature and yearned to be American.

Limits of the "Melting Pot"

It has been America's boast and pride that it absorbed wave after wave of immigrants, including two waves of tens of millions in the early

20th Century, and remained America. The striking metaphor of the "melting pot" emphasized that those who arrived in short order became indistinguishable from other Americans; in college in Cambridge, Massachusetts, my father changed his Polish name from "Dziedzic" to "Donway," becoming, as I used to jest, a good Irish immigrant. Ayn Rand, in one of her unforgettable philosophical clarifications, pointed out that immigrants did not "melt" into an "indistinguishable gray mass" but yielded their national and ethnic identity to the philosophy of American individualism.

In his brilliant *Closing of the American Mind* (Simon & Shuster, 1987), philosopher Allan Bloom gave the "melting pot" a human face:

> ... by recognizing and accepting man's natural rights, men found a fundamental basis of unity and sameness. Class, race, religion, national origin or culture all disappear or become dim when bathed in the light of natural rights, which give men common interests and make them truly brothers. The immigrant had to put behind him the claims of the Old World in favor of a new and easily acquired education. This did not necessarily mean abandoning old daily habits or religions, but it did mean
> subordinating them to new principles. (p. 27)

As I understand it, and feel it, the question confronting America today is if the culture that makes America distinctive, makes it the America we cherish as exceptional, remains potent enough to absorb more millions of immigrants of a different culture? It is by no means a new question. Americans were asking it, with anguished doubt and anger, a hundred years ago, as the millions entered through New York's Ellis Island.

Should we say, as many Objectivists do, that questions about immigrant culture are concrete-bound, a diversion? And that the issue, as Ayn Rand said, again and again, is that a nation's intellectuals must defend its best values, its best ideas, and its political principles. If they do not— and if no "new intellectuals" come forward to do the job—then the ideal, the beacon to mankind, will be extinguished. No cowering together with lovingly preserved traditions, inside border walls, will save the dream. Only philosophy can save us.

But can explicit philosophy, in this case, Objectivism, really keep the best of America's philosophical premises, values, and political traditions alive, if over several decades, America becomes, say, 40 percent Hispanic? (The Pew Research Center reports: "There were 55.3 million Hispanics in the United States in 2014, comprising 17.3% of the total U.S. population. In 1980, with a population of 14.8 million, Hispanics made up just 6.5% of the total U.S. population.") In fact, it may be that only in the America of the time it was published, would *Atlas Shru*gged have achieved the impact that it did. It expressed the specifically American sense of life and glorified the uniquely American achievements and attitudes. It was a novel written for, about, and to the genius of American life.

The Making of One American

Consider what I have written as stating some definitions, terms of discussion, but not pretending to reach a conclusion. What I would like to do is marshal my own personal experience with becoming American, asking what fostered my abiding lifelong consciousness of being part of an American nation. Growing up, what was it that made me feel inalienably part of America, fostered my identity as a citizen, and brought me to adulthood wanting to change nothing essential about America?

If this exercise seems self-congratulatory, perilously parochial, and likely to be bias-confirming, I have this defense: I wish to state only my experience as I see it, now. My goal is to encourage others to state theirs. If, under this weight, my enterprise collapses, so be it.

I return to the statement "wanting to change nothing essential about America." As I got on in life, I met individuals who said they loved America—they just wanted to make America better. They longed for a socialist, welfare-statist America, an America where "communitarianism" replaced individualism, an America that no longer fancied itself "the last best hope of mankind" or "a beacon of freedom." If those things could be changed, America would earn their love. It reminded me of nothing so much as the man who declares imperishable love but would like to change everything about his wife. Archibald MacLeish wrote: "They love not us at all, but love; It is not we but a dream must cover them."

I think of the girl in Leninist Russia who glimpsed America in fleeting images on the movie screen, fell in love with what she saw, risked everything to reach America, and spent her life understanding, affirming, and defending what made America great.

What seems to me (then it is your turn) the roots that yielded my lifelong affirmation that I am an American in America, and proud of it?

■ I was born and raised in a small New England town in a neighborhood of small farms. My parents were born in America, but my grandparents on my father's side came from Poland, on my mother's side from Ireland. No one in our neighborhood was "American" in the May-flower sense. Almost all were second-generation Swedes who flocked to the region to work for the manufacturer, Norton Company. I don't recall, growing up, any friends my age referring to their "heritage." My parents seldom mentioned "roots," although I visited my father's parents regularly and they spoke only Polish. For example, I never knew from what regions or cities in the "old country" my grandparents emigrated. My mother sometimes sang Irish folksongs. I have an indelibly powerful sense of "home" as a landscape, town, and region.

■ Growing up, I knew no one who was not Christian. Our town had New England's great garden of Protestant sects and Catholic churches. My family attended the Congregational Church. The Christian holidays, the songs, the rituals sank deep into my emotions and still linger. But by the time I entered high school, I was an atheist and that has never changed. America itself from the start—including in New England, of course—was an Anglo-Saxon Protestant nation. Those creeds fostered America's profound individualism for 150 years before the Declaration of Independence and the U.S. Constitution. Churches in New England, when I was a boy, had convictions and my mother argued them at Sunday dinner after church. Individualism seemed to prove much stronger than sectarianism; my first wife and present wife are Jewish.

■ My parents were prosperous and entrepreneurial. I knew that their success set me somewhat apart from other children. Can I overlook that materialistic support of my "Americanism"? America, for me, was a good thing and my parents, especially my father, articulated that often: you can be anything you want to be in America. If we had struggled more, done without more often, failed, I might have different feelings about America.

■ No one I met in 12 years of public school spoke anything but English. It would have seemed preposterous to hear anyone claim they must be taught, and speak, anything else. How important was this? My grandparents spoke only Polish; and that is what my father spoke around them. That seemed obvious. I took pride in learning to count to 10 in Polish. Not only English, but American English, and Yankeeisms run very deep in my American identification.

■   In school, we began each day with the Lord's Prayer and the Pledge of Allegiance, the flag always there. That adds up to many thousands of repetitions of the pledge and prayer. I liked it; I liked being part of it.

■   By about my fourth-grade year, television arrived, with just three networks, and spread like a pandemic. How important to my Americanism? On television, back then, "we" seemed much the same: mostly white, English-speaking, patriotic, ever-concerned with America's glorious past, and privileged future. I view the TV westerns as a powerful force for acculturation to America: our past, it seemed, was a story of exploration, heroism, the fight for justice, and good triumphant over evil. I would rate this influence very high in my Americanism. Not least because it coincided with my coming of age to appreciate stories.

■   I grew up in the years immediately following World War II. American arms, the prodigious American economy, and American heroism had triumphed in the world conflagration—indeed, America was the last nation standing. In the wake of that American victory, it seemed, life was all about America: its products, its culture, its influence. No country in modern times had achieved the position of America. I took it for granted, of course; but it was unique in history. I would suggest this triumph of American economic power and American ideals shaped my generation as did nothing else. And I was just in time. By 1960, when I was 16 years old, the bi-coastal internationalist culture and media were scorning American materialism, religion, popular culture, family and sexual values, and America's role in the world. The counter-culture was in full swing; the snarling at American folly had begun. Many, including myself, experience this as a profound loss, a vanished Eden. As generations come of age, now, unfamiliar with this American triumphalism, will their patriotism be the same?

■   I must add, immediately, that, although I grew up with American triumphalism, in the same era, I lived in the almost incomprehensible world of "Dr. Strangelove." A minority of Americans, mostly Jewish immigrant intellectuals from Eastern Europe, were ardent supporters of Soviet communism. But, overwhelmingly, Americans, and American individualism, proved willing to stake everything on winning the Cold War. Living for two decades or more with the daily specter of nuclear war, Americans became (sometimes hysterical) do-or-die patriots.

■   I had graduated from high school, in the summer of 1966, when *Atlas Shrugged* came into my hands. I locked myself in my bedroom, under the eaves, and in three days I read it. When I emerged to eat, I did not speak. When I had finished *Atlas*, whatever loyalty or love I felt for America had become boldly conscious and explicit, now inseparable from my view of knowledge, morality, economics, and politics. In view of what I wrote about the onslaught of the counterculture, my chancing upon *Atlas Shrugged* must rank as near miraculous. It was the very year that I turned 18, an adult, and was preparing to attend a typically liberal college–just as the 1960's cultural revolution got rolling. I began four years of college as though inoculated against the drug culture and hippiedom, New Left anti-Americanism, counter-culture philosophy and esthetics, the explosion of the welfare state and "civil rights," and the patriotic pull of America's first failed war.

■   Although "10" is a nice round number to conclude a list, I make no further points. After encountering *Atlas Shrugged*, my impassioned identification with America—and the ideals that define America—became myself.

> By the rude bridge that arched the flood,
> Their flag to April's breeze unfurled,
> Here once the embattled farmers stood,
> And fired the shot heard round the world…. On
>   this green bank, by this soft stream,
> We set to-day a votive stone;
> That memory may their deed redeem, When,
> like our sires, our sons are gone. Spirit, that
> made those heroes dare,
> To die, and leave their children free…

(Ralph Waldo Emerson's poem written to dedicate the Concord monument on July 4, 1837, commemorating the Battle of Concord, April 19, 1775, the beginning of the American Revolution.)

Published March 28, 2017, by *The Atlas Society*.

Chapter 19

Why Media Networks Cannot Serve "The Public Interest"

We sit by and watch the barbarian. We tolerate him in the long stretches of peace, we are not afraid. We are tickled by his irreverence; his comic inversion of our old certitudes and our fixed creed refreshes us; we laugh. But as we laugh we are watched by large and awful faces from beyond, and on these faces there are no smiles.
— Hilaire Belloc

Thus, we watch or read about the next day the comedian, Stephen Colbert, on one of America's premier *public* television stations, unwinding a roll of toilet paper and joking that the President of the United States is good for nothing but oral sex with Russian Premier Vladimir Putin. That is as far as I am going with describing this. He used the most vulgar vocabulary of sex slang. But I recall a famous ambassador from Israel who said, in an entirely different context: "When you repeat an insult, you insult me all over again."

The reaction of the public suggests that the "barbarian" dared take a long step toward the "inversion" of standards Americans identify as elemental decency. Mr. Colbert tried to go lower; he is the perfect type of self-righteous blowhard who in his rage justifies any means of attacking the object of his hatred. The public explosion of protest at his performance, calls for CBS to fire him, and for viewers to boycott CBS and sponsors of the show, suggest that this is too *big* a step in the final eradication of civility: the declaration that nothing shall be beneath us.

Mr. Colbert has been a productive rising star from a conventional upper-middle-class background, a Roman Catholic born in Washington, D.C., educated in excellent schools, brilliant in climbing the highly competitive ladder in show business. It is not even clear why he became the one to so totally "pull out the stops" on public television, unwinding the toilet paper and uttering savage obscenities about President Trump.

For example, Mr. Colbert chose as the worst insult imaginable his fantasy about homosexual relations involving Mr. Trump. Mr. Colbert remains a practicing Roman Catholic, a Sunday school teacher, and an ordained minister of something called the Universal Life Church Monastery. Mr. Colbert in disguise took the stage at the 2016 Republican National Convention until he was dragged off.

Can we draw a line beyond which the barbarian will not step? It cannot be a limit imposed by government on freedom of speech, which is absolute and inviolable, written into the first amendment to the U.S. Constitution. And it is significant and hopeful that the firestorm of criticism of Mr. Colbert did not call for censorship; it called on CBS to fire Mr. Colbert from the *Late Show* and for a boycott of both CBS and the corporate sponsors of the *Late Show*. Both steps are civil, restrained protests of the grinning, smirking filth that Mr. Colbert flung at America. I certainly endorse them.

You have read how the media, abetted by Democrats, stirred up hatred during the campaign. Its campaign eventually got hysterical thousands out into the streets for violent demonstrations and left a blanket of fear over much of the country. Mr. Colbert is one the dupes of the media who also happens to be self-righteous to the point of convincing himself ANY means are justified by *his* ends. The level of public discourse and civility plunged during the campaign, which the media tried to blame on Trump, but which they fanned and watched smiling as they thought the electorate had bought their story. To then discover that they had not succeeded, even after throwing away truth, ethics, and decency in the name of a higher cause, has led to their crusade to silence the alternative/social/popular media.

Whatever Happened to the FCC?

But I was surprised to see, on *Facebook*, that individuals were registering formal complaints with the Federal Communications Commission (FCC). Yes, the FCC still exists. We don't hear much about it for reasons I intend to explore. And you still can file complaints.

In her first direct communication with readers in the *Objectivist Newsletter*, Ayn Rand urged: "Choose Your Issues!" She identified two urgent public policy issues: The Federal Trade Commission (FTC, responsible, along with the Department of Justice, for enforcing the "antitrust laws") and the Federal Communications Commission (FCC, responsible for regulating the airwaves in "the public interest.") These two agencies, unfortunately as active today as when Ayn Rand wrote in 1962, more than half-a-century ago, still claim to regulate freedom in business and in the promulgation of ideas over the "public airwaves."

Two years later, she continued her criticism of the FCC in "The Property Status of the Airwaves" (April 1964). It is almost incredible, in retrospect, to see the intellectual level of this article. It discussed property rights and how they had been applied in American history (e.g., the Homestead Act of 1862), how the "airwaves" had been discovered and made into "public" property, the philosophy of the right to property in the airwaves, how the philosophy of "public ownership of the airwaves" had evolved since the time of Herbert Hoover; and how the doctrine of the "public ownership" of the airwaves led directly to government control of speech and press on the airwaves, and why this government censorship could not be limited to the airwaves.

There was, she demonstrated, no objective definition of the "public interest" in broadcasting or anywhere else. What could it mean? Consensus? Suppression of disagreement? Instead, she advocated against government licensing of parts of the airwaves spectrum, such as the major TV networks. To make such licenses to an invaluable monopoly dependent upon "serving the public interest" was an invitation to censorship. Or to government "pressure" to broadcast "in the public interest."

The political-philosophical issue identified by Ayn Rand as a priority half-a-century ago has become less visible on today's political scene. We owe this, in part, to a factor identified in her essay: the emergence of new technology must *some extent* made the nature and limits of property in the "airwaves" obsolete. Cable, satellite, Internet: all have made the urgent issue a half-century ago of the "limited" spectrum of the airwaves, and government regulation of airwaves "scarcity," almost a non-issue.

And then, this week, Ayn Rand's emphasis on the impossibility of government's determination of the "public interest" suddenly became urgent when Mr. Colbert said the president of the United States is good for nothing but a homosexual plaything for Russian Premier Vladimir Putin.

The "Public Airwaves" and the "public interest"

CBS is one of the world's foremost television networks, licensed by the United States government. The license, which is "free," is worth tens of billions of dollars, today. In a fascinating Op-Ed for the *New York Times*, Michael J. Copps, one of the five appointed FCC commissioners made matters abundantly clear: 1. Yes, "… America lets radio and TV broadcasters use public airwaves worth more than half a trillion dollars for free. 2. Yes, " .. we require that the broadcasters serve the public interest …" 3. "Using the public airwaves is a privilege—a lucrative one—not a right …"

He then elaborates on the point of his statement, one that has a certain appeal at this point, but would lead to disaster: that the FCC has plenty of leverage, if it wants to exert it, to clean up programming by the broadcast networks. The FCC still renews broadcasters' licenses periodically and is mandated to ensure broadcasters are "serving the public interest." The FCC could act on behalf of Americans to reduce sex and violence in programming, require more educational programming, more coverage of "local civic affairs," support arts and culture, and do better news programming. In other words, as Ayn Rand and other critics of the FCC warned, use the licensing power to enable government to censor and dictate the content of programming.

Mr. Copps laments that this does not happen and explains: The FCC "used to" renew broadcast license holders every three years and scrutinize their "public interest" record. In theory, a broadcasting company could have its license revoked and given to someone pledged to do a better job. Under political pressure from the business conglomerates that now "own" broadcasting companies, the renewal was shifted to every eight years and "Now, we have what big broadcasters lovingly call 'post-card renewal'… Denials on public interest grounds are extraordinarily rare."

In Search of "Decency"

The FCC does still have the mandate to protect standards of "decency" on the airwaves, but that is like defining "obscenity," an issue that has tangled up the Supreme Court for decades. The FCC statement on decency is precisely the convoluted, carefully hedged political document you would expect.

It is a violation of federal law to air obscene programming at any time. It is also a violation of federal law to broadcast indecent or profane programming during certain hours.... the FCC has authority to issue civil monetary penalties, revoke a license, and deny a renewal application. In addition, a federal district court may impose fines and/or imprisonment... The FCC vigorously enforces this law where we find violations, consistent with constitutional and statutory protections of broadcasters' freedom of speech. Beginning in 2006, due to ongoing litigation raising questions about the Commission's indecency standard, the FCC temporarily deferred enforcement action on most indecency cases...

During this period, we have continued to receive and process indecency complaints. In addition, the Enforcement Bureau ("Bureau") has taken steps to reduce the backlog of indecency complaints that resulted from past pauses in enforcement...

The Commission has historically interpreted this [decency] restriction to apply to radio and television broadcasters, and has never extended it to cover cable operators.... viewers of these services have greater control over the programming content that comes into their homes...

Congress and the courts have instructed the Commission only to enforce the indecency standard between the hours of 6 a.m. and 10 p.m., local time, when children are more likely to be in the audience.... the Commission does not act on indecent material aired between 10 p.m. and 6:00 a.m. In this way, constitutionally-protected free speech rights of adults are balanced with the need to protect children...

A "Decent" Definition?

So, what in hell *is* "indecency"? "[U]nder court and agency precedent, the Commission's indecency enforcement is limited to complaints alleging the broadcast of material that describes or depicts sexual or excretory material ...."

Well, at least it sounds as though Mr. Colbert and CBS might have a problem. Well, no, because Mr. Colbert made his remarks on *The Late Show*, after the 6 p.m. to 10 p.m. "safe harbor" period for children. Still enough complaints were made about CBS to the FCC that reporters put the question to FCC Chairman Ajit Pai.

He replied: "It's a free country, and people are willing and able to say anything these days." He added that the Supreme Court had limited the FCC's role in sanctioning broadcasters for their content. And, oddly, he said: "... outside of our decency rules we don't get into the business of regulating content"—a reference apparently to the FCC's only "line in the sand" for "decency" or "the public interest": no explicit sex before 10 p.m. and no "excrement" whatever.

Is it clear by now that to enforce "decency" and "the public interest" is either completely subjective (the FCC today) or dangerous (acting on Mr. Copp's recommendation to get tough about policing content)? In other words, the FCC is giving away licenses to the "public airwaves," for free, to ensure that broadcasters "serve the public interest" but neither setting nor enforcing any standard of "public interest" except daytime sex and excrement.

There Is No "Public Interest"

Because to do so is impossible. Networks simply cannot serve the public interest, because, as Ayn Rand pointed out in 1967, there is no "public interest." Only individuals have "interests"—choices, values, and rights. To seek to enforce a "public interest" is to override the interests of some individuals to serve the interests of others. When government undertakes this task, it does not serve the public interest; it violates individual rights.

Also, the concept of "serving the public interest" in broadcasting rests, in part, on the concept of "the public airwaves," an idea put forth during the administration of Herbert Hoover in the early days of radio and TV broadcasting. Either government authorities could not grasp the nature and requirements of new "property" represented by broadcast frequencies or they approached the issue from a collectivist perspective. Probably both.

The solution, as Ayn Rand explained, was to apply the concept of [private] property to the airwaves. Those whose inventions and investments made broadcasting frequencies economically valuable had literally "made" them property. The perceived "limits" on frequencies were irrelevant; all economic goods are limited. And, as time has shown, the limitation was a matter of the level of technology. Cable and satellite have removed virtually all such limits.

The FCC may have a role, along with the patent office and courts, in objectively defining private property in new communications technology and systems. It may have a role in reviewing interstate systems of communication and standards of connectivity. *May.* Industry groups and associations also could do the job.

But the chief and defining mission that gave birth to the FCC is obsolete—in fact, never was it relevant. The airwaves should be redefined as private property; the broadcast licenses sold to the highest bidder; and government's role in protecting "the public interest" abandoned as it *has been* in all but name.

The private companies that then own the broadcast frequencies will offer viewers whatever they believe viewers will buy. All relevant home technology, in any case, can be programmed to block programs from which parents want to protect their children.

Those who enjoy Mr. Colbert's humor—and look forward to worse, for that is coming, too—or enjoy sex orgies or over-the-top violence or sadism will watch it. Without the convenient myth that government is upholding standards on broadcast television perhaps the public can be made more conscious that *they* must take much more seriously what they tolerate on television, in the movies, in the theater, and in their schools and universities. Because the barbarians who hate middle-class American values and standards of behavior are now pouring through the gates into the citadels of culture where they are shaping new generations of Americans with their Postmodernist rejection of reality, reason, individualism, objective values, and capitalism. I have written about this elsewhere; if you don't understand postmodernist philosophy, you cannot grasp the mindset, motivations, and vision of the America of a Stephen Colbert.

The Barbarians of Postmodernism

But others do understand it, and cheer him on, waiting for what comes next. Notice that the rage stirred up by the media, especially by targeting their often exaggerated or untrue stories to groups such as women, blacks, Latinos, and students, provided cover for leftist thugs to declare *all* their opponents "fascists" and "racists" and so justify violence during the Washington march and other protests and on university campuses to block any speaker they oppose. At the University of California, Berkeley, a notably left-liberal campus and home of the socalled "free speech movement," the shock troops of "anti-fascism" now use violence to exercise veto power over any campus speaker whose views they oppose.

"As we laugh, we are watched by large and awful faces from beyond and on these faces there are no smiles."

Published May 18, 2017, in *The Savvy Street*.

Chapter 20

Still Waiting for America to Become "Intellectually Polarized"

Has the United States become truly and thoroughly "polarized"? Two camps (very broadly speaking) face each other with extreme positions, implacable in their intent to defeat the other, incapable of tolerance for the opposing view, and screaming insults and shaking fists?

If this isn't polarization, what is?

Ayn Rand believed that the answer to that question was fundamental and urgent enough to justify devoting her first issue of *The Ayn Rand Letter* (October 11, 1971) to "Credibility and Polarization."

Almost always, a controversy that won that kind of attention from Ayn Rand involved epistemology—specifically, the nature, pivotal importance, and (often) abuses of concept formation.

"One of their methods," she wrote, speaking of modern intellectuals, "is the destruction of language—and, therefore, of thought and, therefore, of communication—by means of anti-concepts."

An anti-concept is a word attached to a compound of vaguely related examples, an aura of emotional disapproval, and an approximate meaning. It is destructive to clear thought because its intended meaning, what it is meant to convey without naming it, remains implicit. "Polarization" was in vogue, back then, because President Richard Nixon seemed to be challenging the liberal consensus (not very effectively, it turned out!). People no longer conducted their discussions mostly in terms of the "New Frontier," "Great Society," and, going back further, "New Deal" consensus. The liberals had assumed, mistakenly, that that battle had been won permanently with the landslide defeat of Barry Goldwater by Lyndon Johnson in 1964.

The word for this questioning of the consensus—not only of specific policies but of fundamental principles—was "polarization," a term derived from physics denoting "two opposite…principles or tendencies…"

The Anti-Concept of "Polarization"

But, as applied to politics, the term "polarization" was an anticoncept suggesting disunity, dividing the country into warring camps, questioning core political values—and the implication was that such "unbridgeable," "extreme" disagreement might lead to violence and the breakdown of civil society. If we all agreed, then we all would be happy, and there would be no problem, right?

Ayn Rand named the real meaning, or intended message, that the anti-concept of "polarization" was to convey without becoming explicit: "It is principles—fundamental principles—that they are struggling to eliminate from public discussion. It is the clash of fundamental principles that the term 'polarization' is intended to hide and to avert."

In fact, she said, honest political debate can be conducted only in terms of fundamental principles, long-term goals honestly stated, with supporting evidence and projected consequences, honestly discussed. And this kind of 'polarization" was urgently needed. Without it, Americans would plow on through a fog of approximation and deliberate misunderstandings without knowing what was at stake toward a goal they could not identify.

In attempting to clarify what was meant by "polarization," in an article describing it as unprecedented in the 2016 election, *U.S. News* explained: "Public opinion now appears to divide us up to the point that we have a couple of lumps—a liberal lump on one side and a conservative lump on the other." So, that's what's happening!

The *Atlantic* took a shot at describing what was causing "polarization"—you know, lumpiness—in American politics: "The American public is divided—over economic policy, social policy, foreign policy, race, privacy and national security, and many other things. A host of factors, from partisan gerrymandering to exclusionary party primaries, are driving them further apart."

The *Washington Post*, the *Huffington Post*, the Pew Charitable Trust, and dozens of others wondered aloud what could be "dividing America on the issues," but never on "the principles."

It Feels like "Polarization" ...

I explain this at length (no substitute for reading the original, where Ayn Rand introduces herself as "a bromide buster") because today's political debate—and I use that term charitably—feels like "polarization." If "polarization" meant turning Americans implacably against one another, with declarations that ideas one opposes are hopelessly misguided (to put it mildly), then finally we are "polarized" as Ayn Rand described.

But that, of course, is the anti-concept of "polarization." During the Presidential nomination, with the seemingly unstoppable insurgency of Donald Trump, then his election, have we become divided by "...clearcut principles, unequivocal definitions and inflexible goals...the clarifying, reassuring, confidence-and-credibility-inspiring guidance of fundamental principles...intellectual polarization..."? Do I hear giggling?

And yet, I can name several issues with decisive consequences for America that figured into the 2016 campaign from the very start:

■ Mr. Trump pledged to halt all new federal regulations, pending a thorough review of their impact on the economy. (A common figure is that the "drag" on the U.S. economy is $2 trillion a year.

■ Mr. Trump pledged that the scientific hypothesis of apocalyptic "global warming" no longer would guide U.S. energy production away from fossil fuels.

■ Mr. Trump pledged to make appointments to the U.S. Supreme Court of jurists committed to "uphold the Constitution."

■ Mr. Trump pledged to put the safety and interests of Americans before any humanitarian initiatives to admit refugees from countries with active terrorist groups.

By contrast, the Democratic Presidential candidate, Hillary Clinton, now virtually forgotten a month after the election, and Trump's current opponents in the media, did not address principled issues.

■ They did not take up and argue the nature and necessity of economic regulations. They argued (questionable) instances: for example, that any alteration of the Dodd-Frank legislation would put the economy at risk of another financial crisis.

■ They did not argue the principle of governments' worldwide dictating development of the vital energy industry guided by certain scientific speculations. They ran story after story about supposed extreme impacts of changing climate.

■   They did not argue the principle of adherence to the text and historical context of the U.S. Constitution. They talked only about the importance of Roe v. Wade and the unlimited right to abortion.

■   They did not argue the meaning of "America first," but focused on stories about immigrant families and, more recently, travelers inconvenienced by the executive order for review of procedures for screening refugees.

What about Trump's Principles?

But what about Mr. Trump? Did he frame his arguments in terms of "…clear-cut principles, unequivocal definitions, and inflexible goals…"?

No, he offered slogans: "American first," "make America great again," drain the Washington swamp, and uphold the U.S. Constitution. But these are slogans, not principles. Sure, he sounded sort of like an opponent of ever-increasing government power; he sounded sort of like an opponent of out-of-control government spending; and he sounded sort of like an opponent of sacrificing America abroad to non-judgmental acceptance of all cultures and ideologies.

But almost in the same breath, he would speak of stimulating the economy by an epic spending spree on "infrastructure," a kind of mercantilist and protectionist trade policy of government promoting and defending home industries, and a vague commitment to overwhelming military force to crush America's foes, such as ISIS, abroad.

It is an understatement to say that Mr. Trump spoke in terms of dramatic initiatives and inspiring slogans, not political principles. Many listeners apparently got a sense of proposals and promises adding up, in general, to support of capitalism, American prosperity, unapologetic economic growth, and putting American national self-interest first. On the other hand, there always was some proposal suggesting that any principle could be violated in a "good cause."

Republican Presidential candidate Barry Goldwater, in 1964, is remembered for a few statements such as "I do not wish to make government more efficient, for I mean to reduce its size" and "extremism in defense of liberty is no vice…"

I can think of no comparable articulation of principle by Mr. Trump. Only "make American great, again," which, without defining a standard of greatness, Bernie Sanders easily could endorse.

The Sense of Life Alternative

And yet, there remains the belief among Trump supporters that he is a decisive alternative to the liberal-left establishment. His opponents in the media, left-leaning organizations, and the Postmodernist intellectual establishment bolster that belief with their portrayal of "constant crisis" in the new Trump administration. And President Trump, of course, is fighting back against the overwhelming opposition of the media and their tactics—making the media a political issue—as has no other President. I mean, they sure sound as though they are arguing about something that makes a crucial difference!

All of it comes spiked with the confusion resulting, as Ayn Rand wrote, from "meaning (if any) buried under coils of meaningless generalities and safely popular bromides."

Why has the liberal-left freaked out (my first-ever comfortable use of that term because the behavior is freakish—look at Hollywood) at the rise of Trump? I know of no force in our country that could fuel the momentum and fervor of the Trump phenomenon except the American sense of life. It was the final great asset to which Ayn Rand appealed again and again, but she viewed it as dangerously vulnerable because it is emotional, not conceptual and explicit. She asked almost half a century ago: "Is there enough of the American sense of life left in people—under the constant pressure of the cultural-political efforts to obliterate it?" And she answered:

"It is impossible to tell. But those of us who hold it, must fight for it. We have no alternative: we cannot surrender this country to a zero—to men whose battle cry is mindlessness.

"We cannot fight against collectivism, unless we fight against its moral base: altruism. We cannot fight against altruism, unless we fight against its epistemological base: irrationalism. We cannot fight against anything, unless we fight for something—and what we must fight for is the supremacy of reason, and a view of man as a rational being.

"These are philosophical issues. The philosophy we need is a conceptual equivalent of America's sense of life. To propagate it, would require the hardest intellectual battle. But isn't that a magnificent goal to fight for?" ("Don't Let It Go, Part II" The Ayn Rand Letter, Vol. 1, No. 5 December 6, 1971.)

Donald Trump energized that sense of life with his fabled business success in the heart of New York City, his celebration of his wealth, his brashly confident gamble to seize the Republican nomination, his unapologetic lifestyle of glamor, his blunt patriotism, and his feisty "Don't push me around" response to critics. Add to that his unshaken confidence in the face of squalid, literally unprecedented personal attacks by the media—many of them false, out of context, or dependent upon a grotesque double standard. These have made him a paladin of the American sense of life. And if, as Ayn Rand asserted, the last remaining asset of American philosophy is the American sense of life, then Mr. Trump's victories are the re-assertion of that sense of life after the Obama years and faced with the prospect of their continuance by Hillary Clinton.

Of course, this isn't how Trump opponents interpret it. To them, Trump partisans represent extreme and alarming "polarization." He has roused election-winning support with his appeal on issues and with promises—never fully or consistently articulated as principles—that challenge the prevailing liberal-left consensus.

Ayn Rand characterized the state of political discourse in the absence of clearly articulated political principles. The absence of "intellectual polarization," she wrote, makes way for "existential polarization"—pressure group warfare. "The country is splitting into dozens of blind, deaf, but screaming camps, each drawn together not by loyalty to an idea, but by the accident of race, age, sex, religious creed, or the frantic whim of a given moment...by a common hatred of some other group...not by choice, but by terror." Could there be a better description, written as it was in 1971, of contemporary leftist identity politics?

The Job Description of "the New Intellectual"

I became a Trump supporter with many reservations, qualifications, and doubts amid some hope. I could not support Mr. Trump's principles because I could discern no clear principles—only tendencies. In the context of that disclosure, I will assert that I believe the above description of "existential polarization" applies more to the near-hysterical antiTrump forces than to Trump supporters. Throughout the election process the news media and left-leaning organizations and their spokesmen, taking their cue from Clinton, focused on race, ethnicity, sex, disabilities, and religious creed in an uninterrupted series of fabricated "atrocity" stories.

Trump supporters, at times shamed into reticence, retained their excitement at Trump's appeal to the American sense of life. When the day came, they astounded the political pundits and news media by silently, effectively expressing themselves in the polling booth.

It would be a tragedy if President Trump's appeal to the American sense of life, stirring so much resolve and hope—and courage to resist every derogation, from "white nationalist" to "the less educated," to a "basket of deplorables"—led Americans again to the defeat and ignominy of a Watergate. And that is precisely the plan and strategy of the news media and Democratic Party.

Trump's acute vulnerability lies in his failure to articulate and keep emphasizing clear and consistent principles. He does not seem to think in terms of principles, but we can gather that he is for more laissez faire, more limited government under the Constitution, more rule of law, celebration of unlimited economic growth, and genuinely American selfinterest in dealing with other nations. If he could articulate such principles as the context for his initiatives, his opponents would be forced to argue in terms of principles—the fate they have struggled to avoid:

What they dread to discover is the fact that the intellectual status quo that they inherited is bankrupt, that they have no ideological base to stand on and no capacity to construct one.

If they were to articulate the principles behind their policies and actions, those principles would have to include:

■   Collectivism that judges policies and people in terms of group identity—race, sex, "gender," wealth, ethnicity—and communitarianism ("We're all in this together." "You didn't build that.").

■   Statism that views society, through government, as responsible for all problems and for distributing all wealth to solve them.

■   Altruism that views needs as a claim on wealth (e.g., welfare rights).

■   Pragmatism that views all principles, including those embodied in the U.S. Constitution, as "flexible," "evolving," "responsive to change."

■   Anti-Americanism that views America on the world scene as the source of injustices, exploitation, and aggression for which it must atone.

When I was a teenager, working summers during college on my father's housing development, there was an older man, an Irishman from Cork, who had worked like a mule to achieve the American dream—a house, family, schooling for his children, even a car and a small boat—

who used to listen to my polemics, inspired by *Atlas Shrugged,* on the "looters." He responded only briefly, but one succinct comment that I recall was: "Don't let the fuckers get away with it." That depends on us, now.

Published April 8, 2017, on *The Atlas Society.*

Chapter 21

An Appointment with Vouchers

For partisans on both sides of the nomination (and hard-fought confirmation) of Betsy DeVos, 59, of Michigan, as secretary of education, I have glad tidings.

If you long for remission of America's most invasive monopoly—tax-supported ("public") education—Secretary DeVos is your advocate of public-school choice, charter schools, and, above all, vouchers for parents to spend at schools of their choosing. She has been called "a fierce proponent of vouchers" that enable students to attend private schools with public funding. Vouchers for private education would begin to rectify one of the single greatest injustices imposed on American families: paying all their working lives for "free" tax-supported education for other families and then paying all over again for education of their own children at a school of their choosing.

If you are alarmed by her confirmation, there is good news, too. Any significant change she brings to U.S. tax-supported education will come only through voluntary acceptance of her ideas on the local level— the pivotal level of control in American elementary and secondary education. The numbers tell the story. The Budget Office, U.S. Department of Education, reports that "the President's budget request for FY 2017 includes *$69.4 billion* in discretionary funding." And that the Department's "elementary and secondary programs annually serve nearly 16,900 school districts and approximately 50 million students attending more than 98,000 public schools and 28,000 private schools."

The site of the National Center for Education Statistics reports that "*Total expenditures* for public elementary and secondary schools in the United States amounted to *$620 billion...* "

These rudimentary statistics must be considered when assessing the promise or peril of Secretary DeVos. Expenditures for tax-supported elementary and secondary schools in the country are $620 billion a year; the Department of Education spends on all its various programs $69 billion a year.

Thus, the Department spends about one dollar out of eleven that support U.S. elementary and secondary education, both tax-supported and private ("independent" or church supported). But that exaggerates the Department's influence because its budget is fractured into many programs and scattered among tax-supported schools and private schools—a vast and decentralized system.

Opposition to the nomination and confirmation of Secretary DeVos has been near historic. The Senate confirmation vote was 51 to 50, with Vice President Mike Pence breaking the tie—the first time in history this has occurred. The reasons for that historic struggle, if fully explored, would tell the whole story of America's most pervasive monopoly, of government by one-issue factions, and of the willingness of the Trump administration to butcher the holiest sacred cow to feed American children.

DeVos's Resume in Alternatives to Tax-Supported Education

I was discussing the DeVos appointment with a close friend, a respected teacher and program director in New York City schools (taxsupported and independent) for her entire career. The DeVos nomination shocked and angered her. Betsy DeVos, she said, has no connection with public education. And that is the whole extent of the indictment of DeVos in the news media and the flood of letters and phone calls to Congress from the tax-supported education establishment. It kept Democratic senators up all night before the confirmation vote, speaking in the Senate although the outcome of the vote was a foregone conclusion.

That indictment of Secretary DeVos is also the "resume" that recommended her to the new Trump administration. Over the last two decades, she has been arguably the single most diversely experienced, consistent, and influential figure in the experiments in alternatives to taxsupported government education. Certainly, she has not shaded her estimate of the public, tax-supported education monopoly. *The Washington Post* (December 21, 2016) quotes her as saying that tax-supported public education is "a closed system, a closed industry, a closed market. It's a monopoly, a dead end."

The legendary Afro-American commentator, Thomas Sowell, came out of retirement to write an impassioned column in support of DeVos:

"One of the biggest complaints about her is that, unlike Secretaries of Education before her, she does not come out of the government's education establishment. Considering what a miserable job that establishment has done, especially in inner-city schools, her independence is a plus."

My friend argued that "all of this brand-new stuff," such as charter schools, was still experimental and yielded mixed results [unlike the public schools?]. Here, I had to laugh. In the "Objectivist Newsletter," in the late 1960's, Ayn Rand called attention to a brilliant chapter in *The God of the Machine*, in which Isabel Paterson skewered the contradictions and moral dilemmas in tax-supported education that: forces parents 1) to pay for schools that teach ideas they may reject and 2) to send their children to those same schools unless they can afford, in addition to full school taxes, the cost of tuition at a private school.

At that time, any principled opposition to tax-supported education was heresy; it was, and is, the bedrock collectivist ideal. It embodies the collectivist concepts of "rights"—the "right to education"— egalitarianism—the "right" to an equal education—the responsibility of the state—"to educate all citizens"—and conformity to the collective ideal—education as the "seedbed of democracy."

The altruist defense of tax-supported public education is not original: "So, it's all right if children grow up totally illiterate?" is the equivalent of "So, it's all right if people are dying in the streets?" Already, as that argument was mounted, states were creating vast systems of higher education subsidized by taxpayers and demanding the right of every American to tax-supported higher education. And so, the collectivists exposed the hypocrisy of their own "illiterate children" argument and revealed their goal. It is considered, today, passé to call that goal "socialized education," just as it is viewed as "retro" to refer to "socialized medicine."

Getting at the Issue: Force or Choice

But that is what it is. Ayn Rand pointed out that the totalitarian nature of government education in America was partially obscured by the continued existence of private schools supported by parents so committed to the best education for their children that they are willing to pay twice.

If parents do not rebel at this, asking "If my children do not use the schools, and so occasion no expense, why am I paying full-fare in school taxes?" it is because of altruism. To protest at paying for the education of other children, even while paying for my own, is viewed as selfish. When Ayn Rand advocated, as an "emergency measure," a response to the public-education vice, she named specifically tax-credits for education— a variant on vouchers.

Independent and parochial schools are a major sector of education through the high-school level. They have thrived for decades despite competition from "free schools." It is preposterous to claim that there is no viable alternative to the tax-supported cartel. The alternative has exemplified robust competition and market appeal. (Indeed, an issue faced by all private schools is what percentage of their class to admit from abroad, where "full-pay" parents worldwide clamor to gain admission for their children.)

Today, with our massive tax-supported school system, a transition to private and independent schools will be required. Vouchers embody a commitment to guarantee universal elementary and secondary education, but take government out of the business of designing, running, and evaluating schools. It is a policy prescription that addresses both the moral issue (the injustice of paying twice) and the fatal weakness of any enterprise protected by law from competition. (The latter is the essential argument for school choice within the tax-supported system.)

Vouchers for education go back at least to 1869, in Vermont, where districts were too small to have high schools. In the 1960s, they were used in some southern states to enable parents to avoid forcibly integrated schools. I predict that if vouchers become a major controversy, you will be treated to documentaries revisiting that brief, unfortunate period. But the rising Nazi Party in Germany used documentaries to glorify the regime. So, let's not have any more documentaries?

The political pressure for vouchers is less than you would expect. Local school districts across America propose an annual budget, subject to community vote. Districts tax families to pay, often very generously, for schools. Often, though not always, those families control the schools;

and the level of public education is adequate to outstanding. These parents pay school taxes and their children attend the schools. In this way, a great many families avoid paying twice.

Where to Spend the Money

Families who need vouchers are those seeking better schools than their district offers and must face private school costs in addition to school taxes. And the *desperate* need for vouchers is by families in the many districts in the inner-city and some rural areas with failing schools. Too often, the schools fail because the neighborhoods do not work— because the culture does not work. The dysfunctional culture is a problem education can address; but education does not work in the dysfunctional culture. That is why, half-a-century and trillions of dollars after the launching of the "Great Society" and the "War on Poverty" in 1968, we hear the same complaints about the same problems—only worse

Where should Department of Education dollars be spent? Enlarging the voucher system, consistent with the new Secretary's convictions, or divided among all schools? This is where philosophy transitions into policy because philosophy can offer no principle for deciding. Private conscience is a right of private wealth; but it is mere bias, a threat to the "consensus," where tax dollars are at stake.

We do know that compromise with this ethical dilemma has driven the creation of alternatives to the public-school monopoly: 1) schools-ofchoice, which permit parents to apply to public schools outside their own district, including "magnet" schools, and 2) the "charter school" movement through which parents and teachers, and sometimes education entrepreneurs, can obtain tax support for new schools. DeVos in recent years has led both movements.

If she directs funds to paying for vouchers, she will relieve some parents of double payment and support private schools, but those parents will continue to pay taxes for public education, which will remain unchanged. If she directs funds to schools of choice and charter schools, she is investing, for the most part, in reforms within the tax-supported system.

We must wait to see what Secretary DeVos will make of this opportunity. It is one that I had not even hoped might be offered to a secretary of education in my lifetime. As a kind of illustration of the policy choices available to DeVos, let me suggest only one way to react.

Mr. Trump made daring promises to residents of America's impoverished inner-city neighborhoods. These families are enduring the disaster of tax-supported education; they desperately need a way out of schools tied to their neighborhood and culture.

DeVos could devote substantial funds to vouchers for these families. The children would attend private schools, including boarding schools. She should prevail upon boarding schools to provide board in exchange for full-tuition payments. Get the students out of their neighborhoods and into effective schools.

This is also a political strategy. Yes, federal education dollars would be going for vouchers, not to tax-supported schools. But vouchers would be going to the certified neediest students, mostly minority, and tax-supported public schools are relieved of the cost of educating those students, but with no loss of revenue. After four years, perhaps eight, tens of thousands of "inner-city" kids will have attended private schools and the evaluation will reveal that the experience was transformative. Some thousands of inner-city (mostly African-American) youths will be educated, articulate advocates of the private education system. This could go a long way toward undercutting the argument that any change in taxsupported education will hurt the most vulnerable students.

That is simply an illustration of the kinds of choices available to the new Secretary of Education.

Count on the ideological ferocity of public school bureaucracy in denying any accomplishment that casts doubt on their monopoly. For them, the only choice is socialism in education versus a kind of anarchy that they never define. The anarchy they mean is lack of any dominant, legally-enforced system operated by licensed government employees to dictate how and what Americans will learn.

For collectivists, that is "anarchy." For Secretary DeVos, apparently, it is freedom.

Published February 23, 2017, on *The Atlas Society*.

Chapter 22

Ideology in Drag: Al Gore's Truth Is "Convenient" Anti-Capital-ism

Sitting in a theater on Saturday. I watched two or three previews of coming films, including one sci-fi apocalypse, and was commenting to my wife about "addiction to terror" and "minimal acceptable catastrophe" when the next preview began. Great cities swept away in floods, hurricane-flattened landscapes, tidal waves, incinerating wildfires, seas roiled with plunging ice cliffs...

What is *this*? Oh…well, since that heavy set, grim-faced man yelling at the viewer about "truth," "morality," and "democracy" is former U.S. Vice President Al Gore, and that brief cartoon sequence of a buffoon is supposed to be the President of the United States, Donald Trump, this must be…*An Inconvenient Sequel*.

Yes, the new movie previewed at the Sundance Film Festival in January is coming to theaters and picking up where *An Inconvenient Truth*, a 2006 Oscar-winning documentary on Al Gore's crusade for recognition and action on "global warming," never left off. No, never left off; that film is shown and taught in schools throughout the English-speaking world to terrify (or is it titillate?) students with the distinct impression that their planet soon will look like the best special-effects apocalypse.

A British High Court judge ruled on a suit to stop the film from being used in public schools after the government sent a copy to every secondary school in the country. The judge declared the film "exaggerated and alarmist," calling attention to nine specific errors including the claim that ocean levels might soon rise as much as 20 feet (the U.N. International Panel on Climate Change, or IPCC, estimated less than two feet over a century). The judge took pains to declare that the film was "broadly accurate," but, in contrast to the nine specific errors offered no argument. We will examine below how easy it was for the judge to offer that consolation.

An Inconvenient Truth was widely hailed as among the most urgent documentaries of our time. The film won Gore the Nobel Peace Prize in 2007, awarded jointly to the IPCC, and leading to a humorous interlude where the head of the IPCC informed the literally hundreds of contributors to its annual reports that they *all* could describe themselves as "Nobel laureates." This scam, finally quashed by the Nobel organization, is alltoo-typical of how "climate science" operates, today.

Exactly Who *Are* These "Global-Warming Deniers"

I am viewed as a "global warming denier," which accounts for the tone, so far, of this article. Except, I *don't* deny "global warming. A report in 2013, tirelessly quoted, said that 97 percent of climate scientists affirmed the reality of global warming. This was based not on a poll of scientists but a review, by staff of the Web site "Skeptical Scientist," of papers on global warming by scientists. The scientists were not informed or consulted; the staff members simply rated the papers. To be a global warming affirmer, a scientist had to assert or imply that Earth's atmosphere traps heat from the sun that increases the Earth's average global temperature. I agree. Without our atmosphere, which holds in heat, our planet would be a dead ice ball spinning through space. A scientist had to assert that the Earth's atmosphere included carbon dioxide, which contributes to trapping heat from the sun. I agree. Carbon dioxide is a one of the trace gases making up about one percent of the atmosphere (the chief gases are oxygen and nitrogen).

A scientist had to assert that man's activities ("anthropocentric" causes) generated carbon dioxide. I agree. All burning of carbon-based fuels (woods, coal, oil), and all oxidation involved in breathing, rusting, rotting, defecating, produces carbon dioxide. The Earth's oceans, land, and lower atmosphere have hundreds of billions of tons of carbon dioxide. The U.S. Environmental Protection Agency estimates that at present some 3.7 percent of new CO_2 is contributed by human activities.

Fourth and finally, a scientist had to assert that the 3.7 percent of

CO_2 produced by man's activities, like the other CO_2 and gases in the atmosphere, contributes to the "greenhouse effect"—our atmosphere's trapping heat from the sun that warms the average surface and ocean temperatures. I agree. So, I score 100 percent "agreement" with "global warming."

And there you have the "97 percent of climate scientists" who "agree with global warming." That means *nothing* about the claims of today's "global warming" crusade, which is better labeled "Big Climate Alarmism" or the "Climate Catastrophe Movement." This movement asserts that the contribution of manmade CO_2 to the atmosphere *since the Industrial Revolution* (we will see why *this* is the single most crucial premise of the movement) is making a relatively small but decisive contribution of new CO_2 to the atmosphere. This new CO_2, produced by human use of virtually all current energy sources, is creating a global warming not of unprecedented *size* (that idea eventually was shot down) but unprecedented speed—a rapidity associated with previous "global extinction events."

Greening While We Await the Apocalypse

Not now, of course, but in perhaps 50 to 100 or more years. Glaciers and the Earth's frozen poles will melt; the seas will rise, flooding cities and whole countries; acidification of the oceans will kill sea life; the Earth will parch to desert, killing greenery and becoming tinder for apocalyptic wildfires; all natural catastrophes from hurricanes and tornados to tidal waves will magnify....

Right now, the only proven global effect of increased CO_2 is that the Earth's wild greenery, including all crops, have had a nice surge, with a one-third increase in the entire planet's green cover. One of many misrepresentations by Gore and others is to refer to "pollution" of the planet. They know better. Through the process of photosynthesis, CO_2 is plant food: indeed, the chief plant food. Scientists who deny Big Climate Alarmism point out that even today the Earth is relatively CO_2 starved; earlier periods of lush tropical growth and proliferation of species have had more CO_2 in the atmosphere (as revealed by studies of historical trace levels in fossils, ice cores with levels from earlier geological eras).

The New Left Re-Invents Anti-Capitalism

One of Ayn Rand's most prescient analyses of trends, and projections of the future, came in her essays about the nascent 1970's environment movement and its philosophical substratum "ecology." In a series of essays, later compiled as *The New Left: The Anti-Industrial Revolution*, she identified the "green" ideology movement as the historical successor to the Old Left's chief thrusts against capitalism.

She wrote that Marxism first claimed, in the name of the international proletariat, that capitalism caused endless wars fought by the proletariat for the interests of the capital class. But WWI and WWII showed that wars were launched by statist governments such as Kaiser Wilhelm's Germany, National Socialist Germany, fascist Italy, and the Japanese Empire against the freer capitalist nations of the United States France, and Britain. (Only after trying desperately to join with Hitler in the early days of WWII, and being turned on by Hitler, did Joseph Stalin's Russia join the Allies.

The next Marxist attack on capitalism was that it impoverished workers, progressively worsening their wages and working conditions to build capital. But the example of America, Britain, and all nations with a market economy made abundantly clear that everyone in these economies prospered, enjoying prosperity that remained a dream under socialism.

And now, wrote Rand, as the so-called "environmental movement" gained headway, the attack of the New Left was that capitalism was polluting our air and water, exhausting our natural resources, and making a mess of the wilderness. Overwhelmingly, the liberal/left took this seriously. During the 1970's, a supposedly "conservative" President Richard Nixon signed the National Environmental Policy Act and created the Environmental Protection Agency. Costs to businesses of complying skyrocketed in that decade and never have looked back. With the Obama administration's gargantuan regulation and spending packages aimed at "climate change," environmental regulations alone, the Competitive Enterprise Institute estimates, cost $1.8 trillion a year, including $55.4 billion by government (taxpayers) for regulatory administration and policing. CEI points out that those regulation costs exceed total 2008 corporate pretax profits of $1.436 trillion and tower over estimated individual income taxes of $936 billion (Reported in *Forbes*.)

Although at the cost of trillions in investment capital, capitalism succeeded in producing and implementing technological solutions to every form of actual pollution. But the demand to invest in ever-more rigorous protection of water, air, special habitats, 'wilderness, and "oceans" never lessened, only the problems themselves lessened. In the United States today, water and air quality, preservation of "wilderness," protection of endangered species, and every other environmental goal has achieved and exceeded initial goals repeatedly.

But, for the environmental ideologists, of course, clean air and clean water, protection of endangered lizards and owls, were never the goals. The goal was to indict capitalism and the Industrial Revolution per se. That ideological goal has not changed; only the nature of the attack on capitalism. The left has learned from its earlier defeats. The "disaster" that capitalism will cause has been pushed out a century or more. But *now* is the time to shut down the entire fossil-fuel industry worldwide that provides energy for the modern economy.

The environmentalists usually don't say so, of course; they advocate new energy sources that are "natural"—i.e., untainted by man's manipulations. Wind and solar power require only use, no *change* in the Earth such as mining, drilling, piping, burning. Man, the species that does not adapt to nature to survive—the species that changes the Earth to meet his needs—now must renounce reason, knowledge, science, technology, and industrial production. He must cease to be the metaphysical freak of the universe.

A Convenient Conceptual Chaos

Now, you would like the short list of "knockdown" arguments demonstrating that Big Climate Alarmism is not science, but ideology. But you should be aware that, as always, the *burden of the proof* is on those who assert a positive: that potentially catastrophic global warming *is* occurring and what its consequences will be over a given time.

Scientists who question the "global warming" scenarios are not predicting what Earth's climate will be like in 2050 or 2100. They are asserting that what the Earth's climate will be next spring is difficult and chancy to predict; the far longer projections of Big Climate Alarmism are unsubstantiated, often self-contradictory, frequent proved wrong when they have been short term. Their methodology, especially more than 100 global climate models, failed them in predicting a change in climate trend in 1998, never mind 2098, and so on. Despite billions of taxpayer dollars spent on "climate research," none of it going for work of scientists questioning the tenets of Big Climate Alarmism, and despite systematic attempts to destroy the careers of scientists who are labeled "global warming skeptics," Big Climate Alarmism has not made its case.

I did take up some arguments in "Why I Deny Big Climate Alarmism," which I enlivened with personal stories and humor. I recommend it as an adjunct to this article and as a source of references for reading.

No one can give you an honest state-of-the-art assessment of climate science. Not anymore. The entire field, once struggling toward credibility (I mean, making weather predictions for next weekend more reliable), is now a political arena where the global gladiatorial forces of capitalism and the Industrial Revolution clash in combat with the forces of environmentalism and the anti-Industrial Revolution.

What other physical science, today, can make no single assertion that is not challenged by other scientists as not only false, but dishonest? "Climate science," as it is called, although it is an amalgam of studies from astrophysics (the now-denied role of the sun's changes in the climate) to energy economics (the new "energy poor" in Europe as non-carbon energy sources cause prices to skyrocket), has virtually no agreed principles—except, perhaps, the high-school physics of "global warming" that I have reviewed.

The methods of science are examination of a hypothesis by reference to observations, experiments, appeal to facts and logic. Rarely, in modern times, has a science's every deliberation been slugged-out in media headlines, involved orations by politicians and actors, launched marches to Washington, assembled the world's politicians to affirm the science and act in concert, and become a dispute in a U.S. Presidential election. Those are manifestations not of the discussion of science but of political ideology. The dispute today over "global warming" wears the mask of science but has the face of ideological warfare.

The "March to Silence" Dissent

April 22 was Earth Day, which now focuses not on the Earth but "the Earth's atmosphere and pollution." This year, the day featured a mass march on Washington, D.C., where a new President has ignited fury and terror in crusaders for Big Climate Alarmism. A typical speaker was Neil deGrasse Tyson, host of a popular TV show and director of the Hayden Planetarium at the Museum of Natural History, who said that the Trump administration's failure to embrace climate alarmism is a "threat to informed democracy."

Meanwhile, also on April 22, an Earth Day "March for Science" passed the University of Alabama, Huntsville, during the afternoon. As night fell, seven shots were fired from the street at the National Space Science and Technology building. All seven hit the building's fourth floor, where John R. Christy has his offices.

Christy is a particularly annoying skeptic of Big Climate Alarmism because of his credentials. Dr. Christy is the distinguished professor of Atmospheric Science and director of the Earth System Science Center at the University, where he began studying global climate issues in 1987. Since November 2000, he also has been Alabama's State Climatologist.

The report so far is that police summoned to the scene concluded that his was a "random shooting"—that is, with no intended target or victim. Just seven pot shots at a building, clustering around one floor. As a result, the story got *no* coverage in media reports about Earth Day. A colleague of Prof Christy did make this Report:

All bullets hit the 4th floor, which is where John Christy's office is...

Given that this was Earth Day weekend, with a March for Science passing right past our building on Saturday afternoon, I think this is more than coincidence. When some people cannot argue facts, they resort to violence to get their way. It doesn't matter that we don't "deny global warming"; the fact we disagree with its seriousness and the level of human involvement in warming is enough to send some radicals into a tizzy...

Maybe the "March for Science" should have been called the "March to Silence" [dissenting scientists].

Chapter 23

Not the Leader They Want Us to Follow

What is the focus of U.S. politics, today? Or, if "focus" is too mild an expression, what is today's *obsession* in politics? I would suggest to you that it is "leadership": the qualifications, character, honesty, family, style, and latest Tweets of the President of the United States.

To read the print and broadcast media is to encounter a daily assessment, frankly editorial or, more frequently, editorial presented as news, of what Donald Trump has said or done. (In addition to the requisite hourly report on the progress of investigations of the White House by Trump's political opponents.)

Recent news focused on President Trump's visit to the Middle East to navigate the dangers of Islamic fundamentalism, U.S. military intervention, the Israeli-Palestinian conflict, and, later, the role of the North Atlantic Treaty Organization (NATO) in defending Western interests in the region.

Fake News

A remarkable number of stories were what have been called "fake news." One breathless report was that the President's wife, Melania, subtly declined to hold his hand as they approached welcoming Israeli officials. And every major news outlet ran a story that Trump may have "elbowed" aside the prime minister of Montenegro in moving, as requested, to the front row for the official photo of NATO leaders. The bewildered prime minister of Montenegro, which is applying for NATO membership, denied any "pushing" toward the front row and sputtered, "But he is President of the United States!" Other stories focused on (just the latest of many) "corruption" investigations—this time of Trump's Jewish son-in-law.

Fascism as Leaders with Unlimited Power

In an article ("The Fascist New Frontier" in *Capitalism: The Unknown Ideal*) that permanently changed our understanding of socialism, Ayn Rand, in a startling comment on the Kennedy administration, wrote: "The difference between [socialism and fascism] is superficial and purely formal, but it is significant psychologically: it brings the authoritarian nature of a planned economy crudely into the open."

She then elaborated: At the heart of "socialism" is a utopian collectivist plan, including government "ownership" of the means of production, that promises that sometime in the undetermined future, after decades of sacrifice for the "common good," there will blossom an economy of permanent, universal prosperity. In contrast: "The fascistNazi axis merely extols *leadership*—leadership without purpose, *program* or direction—and power for power's sake." [emphasis added]

The entire 2016 U.S. election campaign, as framed by the mainstream media, focused up candidate Trump as a potential leader. Scant attention was called to his rather surprisingly pro-market and
"America first" proposals.

-- Slash corporate taxes to keep America a competitive place to do business.

-- Defund the "global warming/climate catastrophe" movement and extend genuine free enterprise to the energy industry.

-- Drastically reduce regulations that today are an estimated twotrillion-a-year drag on the U.S. economy.

-- Repeal and replace the Obama administration's giant step toward full socialized medicine, the Affordable Care Act ("Obamacare").

-- Enforce U.S. statutes on immigration that have been violated by tens of millions of illegal entrants from Mexico and elsewhere in Central America.

-- Unleash the military might of the United States and its allies against violent Islamic jihadism, especially the Islamic State in Iraq and Syria (I.S.I.S.).

Ayn Rand wrote, in the same article: "The fascist-Nazi axis offers nothing but loose talk about some unspecified form of *racial* or *national* "greatness." Notice, four months into the Trump administration, how his political opponents, the media, and the liberal-left intellectual and academic world *frame* this issue. Their target is not Trump's slogan: "Make America Great Again." Because, as shown above, Trump was often specific about the form that "greatness" should take and the policies implied. Those proposals are strictly secondary, if even that, in what his opponent attack.

Making President Trump's Leadership the Issue

No, their focus is upon his personality as a leader of what they view as America's m*oral* destiny (e.g., altruism, egalitarianism), *cultural* destiny (e.g., "multi-culturalism," a focus on "injustice" to minorities, sexual/gender polymorphism), *political* destiny (e.g., income equality, focused on conversion to a "green" economy), and *internationalist* role (e.g., open borders, refugees rescue, sacrificing to poverty worldwide). When his opponents, including the media, are not seeking legal grounds to impeach the President, their entire focus is upon his *failure in this leadership* (or to put it another way, his poverty of "political correctness").

These are a few recent headlines from leading liberal-left media:
"Trump's Draft Plan to Cut off Food Stamps for Immigrants Could Cause Some U.S.Citizens to Go Hungry" (*Washington Post*, February 3)
"Trump Care's Cruelty: Reaffirmed" (*New York Times*, May 27)
"Donald Trump: The Gateway Degenerate…" (*NYT*, May 29)
"The Awkward Body Language of Donald Trump" (*NYT*, May 26)
"Donald Trump's Racial Ignorance" (*NYT*, Dec. 3, 2016) "Donald Trump's Unamerican Refugee Policy" (*NYT*, Jan. 27)
"The End of Foreign Aid as We know it" (*Foreign Policy*, Apr. 24)
"Trump Budget Slashes Climate Change Funding" (*NPR*, Mar. 16)
"Implicit Sexism Trump Displayed with Merkel" (*NYT*, Mar. 21)
"Ivanka Trump's Dangerous Fake Feminism" (*NYT*, Jan. 13)
"America Inequality Will Widen Under Trump" (*Reuters*, Dec. 29, 2016)
"Trump's Preposterous Rationale for Revoking Transgender Bathroom Rights" (*Washington Post*, Feb. 24) "Trump's Stupid and Reckless Climate Decision," *NYT*, June 2.
"Trump Is Abdicating All the Country's Moral Power," *Washington Post*, June 2.

Trump's approach "asserts that selfishness is the sole driver of human affairs…" *NYT*, June 3.

"Powerful, selfish people [like Trump and his top advisors] have always adopted this dirty-minded realism to justify their own selfishness." *NYT*, June 3.

These are a few among literally thousands of "news" stories, editorials, and opinion columns that indict Trump's leadership. If I were to stoop to quoting Hollywood celebrities on Mr. Trump, the mask of journalistic seriousness would come off and the totally personal nature of the attacks would become clear.

Oh, well, maybe just a few because today (May 31), the President seemed by implication to say he would withdraw the United States from the Paris Accords on climate. Hollywood exploded, if you can explode with Tweets:

Cher: "To people of the world. Know that there are millions of us being held hostage by insane DICTATOR!! He trashes American values & admires killers!"

Mark Ruffalo: "If this is true he will have the death of whole nations on his hands. People will be looking to the USA for retribution for what they loose." [He means "restitution" and "lose."]

Don Cheadle: "If you care about your kids maybe reconsider your Paris Accords decision. Barron will thank you when he sees you, whenever that is."

Alec Baldwin: "The President is such a senile idiot all he has is Tweet fights."

We see an obsessive focus on political correctness, the right *spiritual leadership* of America. That intensity of focus implies that social and political conformity are the very *minimal* basis of American life. As Ayn Rand suggested some half-a-century ago, the ideal of fascism is not economic or even political. It is that *leadership* will define and enforce a nation's collective direction and spirit--how and where "the people" march. With his celebration of the values and aspirations of Middle America, his business fortune and enjoyment of wealth, his characteristic masculine assertiveness and emphatic heterosexuality, and his seeming insensitivity to the increasingly frantic media-Hollywood campaign denouncing him, Donald Trump is a nightmare to the political-cultural postmodernists. And the icy shock is even more painful after the 100 percent politically correct, super-cool, unfailingly "progressive" Barrack Obama.

Trump and the People He Leads

We can't predict if making Trump-as-leader their battleground will achieve for his opponents what they impatiently anticipate: his being forced out of office. Most of them want nothing less. Concessions on policies, programs, and even principles won't satisfy them because what irks them is the spirit of America and the American sense of life. Trump cannot continue Obama's leadership toward an egalitarian, multicultural, postmodernist, internationally unexceptional, increasingly "green," politically correct America defined in terms of collective agendas: racial, ethnic, egalitarian, LGBT, feminist, and "challenged."

His opponents won't come out and say it, but they see Trump as from the same mold as the middle Americans who put him in office: focused on their own economic future, more excited about cheap energy than "green" crises, stolidly bourgeois in their view of marriage and family, unabashedly religious, insensitive to exploited minorities from women to gays to Black teenagers, and childishly patriotic about
America's "greatness" as a world power and a force for good.

The adults among them probably are written off as hopeless, but with the right leadership in the White House--government agencies committed to the agenda of Greenpeace--support for thousands of politically correct groups from the humanities and the arts to science-steady pressure on the public schools to pursue the right "social agenda"-the reliable crusade of colleges and universities for postmodernism in all fields—the *children* of the Trump-supporting "deplorables" might follow the right leaders, which the media will identify for them.

Then, at last, will the humiliation and rage suffered by the liberal left in the 2016 election be exorcised.

Conclusion: Postmodernism Versus Civilization

It is difficult to believe that one-eighth of President Trump's term already is history. So far, it is a "history" that lacks genuinely dramatic moments: no new wars, no new Jihadist outrages delivered upon the homeland. We have had to settle for "crises" such as the hundred or more immigrants delayed at airports by the temporary ban and the ensuing angry demonstrations; the U.S. withdrawal from the Paris Accords on climate control to cries that Trump is "murdering" the planet; North Korea's malevolent advance toward full status as a nuclear power; and Congressional efforts to revise or repeal and replace ObamaCare.

After the climactic alarm and warnings of domestic chaos and global peril during the election, the reality has been tame. What *has* continued, though, is an air of crisis as Congress and the media daily scan a menu of suitable grounds for impeaching the President, seeking some footing for another Watergate. The other theater of crisis is the media opinion pages. The latest issue of *The New Republic* leads off with half a-dozen stories about President Trump: e.g., dangerously isolated by his populist politics, dangerously surrounded by supine family and political toadies, and dangerously failing to appoint "inspector generals" and so sidestepping scrutiny.

Following that line up is a big story, some eight full pages, devoted to how an outreach facility in Bangladesh operated by an evangelical Christian charity has had a case of sexual abuse by a religious staff member. You *do* get the connection? Christian evangelicals heavily supported and voted for Trump and, well, so much for *their* self-righteousness! Perverts!

I would be remiss, not to mention open to criticism, to omit comment on another article in the same issue. It is long and detailed, heavily documented, and charges that, since Trump, the Left has let a thousand conspiracy theories bloom in sheer desperation to expel Trump from the body politic. The article documents the wild speculations about Trump-inspired assassination of Russian dissidents, Trump acting under pressure of Russian blackmail, secret Russian funds pouring into Trump accounts. The taxonomy of species of conspiracy and their characteristic logical fallacies is impressive. One conclusion? Well, lack of evidence doesn't prove the speculations are *untrue*. Who knows? We can hope.

Themes seen during the nomination, election, and inauguration are being elaborated. At first, they appeared to be overshadowed by the drive to overturn the election results and then for impeachment, the preferred charge being the one that brought down Richard Nixon, "obstruction of justice"—notoriously difficult to defend against for an individual at the apex of *all* law enforcement. So, we had the headlines about a dinner conversation between FBI Director James Comey and President Trump— and Trump's later decision to fire Comey allegedly for insufficient "loyalty."

After Congressional testimony by Comey and other national security executives, which produced yards of newspaper copy but no evidence of obstruction of justice by the President, my perception is that the drive to criminalize the President's involvement with Russia is pooping out. That is occurring, in part, because of lack of new revelations or evidence for older ones; but you can't overlook that this President, as no other in present memory, has gone after the media with fierce directness, pointing to "fake news," "false allegations," and naming names of publications and reporters. Inevitably, given the standards of Postmodern journalism, and the *daily* production of attacks, some of the President's charges have been proven indisputably true. Then, the President himself, and, of course, his supporters, have turned the attack, pursuing the retreating forces with vindictive verve. All this is *new* in degree, though not in kind, in contemporary American politics.

For reasons like these, reporting in the mainstream media has moderated significantly. A state of crisis cannot be sustained indefinitely. It becomes the norm. The peak of fear, anger, and combativeness stirred up especially in women, and the impulse to flood into the streets to protest, require fresh and ever-greater fuel and the Trump administration has not provided it. *The New Republic* is alarmed that Trump has left unfilled the post of "inspector general" in more than a dozen departments and agencies (so did Obama). But you cannot use that to get mobs into the streets.

The violence of the self-styled "anti-fascists," which shut down free speech by invited Trump advocates at the University of California, Berkeley, also is less in evidence. But perhaps the speakers are less in evidence. We shall see.

Professional intellectuals such as Charles Murray, Ann Coulter, and even Milo Yiannopoulos are not going to go away. How many times will the black-masked "Antifasc" demonstrators be bused to Berkeley to silence them? Nevertheless, like a slamming echo of that violence, there was the attempted mass murder of Republican Congressman Steve Scalise, aides, and police on June 14 in Alexandria, Virginia. The gunman was distraught over Trump's election.

The first pay-offs

Meanwhile, those who elected the President are seeing at least some results that must please them. These are not legislative victories; it is too soon, for that. They are the kind of decisions I said, from the very beginning of Trump's campaign, could slow the momentum of Left-Liberalism across the board. One such decision, of course, was nomination in March of a new Supreme Court justice, Neil Gorsuch, hailed as epitomizing the type of judge who decides cases based on the Constitution. Another decision, which had for many Trump supporters the quality of a dream-come-true, was announcement on June 1 that the United States would withdraw from the Paris Climate Agreement—a defeat for the forces of the "anti-Industrial Revolution."

There have been dozens of directives and executive orders freeing specific sectors of American life: farming, coal mining, drilling for energy, enforcement of immigration laws, banking and finance, energy, and, of course, decision-making about bathrooms. At the essence of all these is ending regulations.

Cause to cheer

Just yesterday, July 5, traveling in Europe, President Trump addressed the Polish people at the site of the WWII Warsaw Ghetto uprising. He rejected multi-culturalism, albeit in the name of Western culture broadly, asserting the limits to immigration that may rapidly and radically alter Western civilization:

"We must work together to confront forces that threaten over time to undermine our values and erase the bonds of culture, faith, and tradition."

"...the defense of the West ultimately rests not only on means but also on the will of its people to prevail. The fundamental question of our time is whether the West has the will to survive?"

"Do we have the confidence in our values to defend them at any cost? Do we have enough respect for our citizens to protect our borders? Do we have the courage to preserve our civilization in the face of those who would subvert and destroy it?"

It was appropriate to speak first of defense of our "values" and "our civilization"—specifically alluding to free speech, history, music, art, and science—and then of "bonds" of culture, faith, and tradition. It would have been still better to speak of the philosophical *ideas* that defined and upheld, in the West, reason, individualism, human rights, the rule of law, and governments strictly and in principle limited by a constitution—leaving free human activity in fields from production and trade to thought and expression to religion.

But I suggest to you that the President's words, in this context and setting, with this degree of passion and specificity, are *precisely* what his supporters endured so much to assert at the polls on November 8. The deliriously excited Polish crowds that greeted Trump's words, chanting his name repeatedly, may reinforce for him and his advisors the importance to his supporters of values as deep as Western civilization itself.

When he spoke of "forces that threaten over time to undermine our values," he went on to refer to "radical Islamic terrorism" and "mass immigration." Those are not threats that he deflected with his victory on November 8. But if the challenge that he *did* deflect, Postmodernism's assault on reason and individualism, is not defeated on its own battleground--philosophy, ideas, and education—then no other victory, however grand, will save American civilization or the West.

"And his enemies"

The Warsaw speech, already being called the "Trump Doctrine," is an uplifting conclusion for this book. But our thesis is the importance, for understanding Trump's electoral victory and its importance, of his *enemies*. They have not gone away.

The day after the speech, Trump and his wife were in Hamburg, Germany, for a meeting of the G20 countries. Melania Trump could not attend the opening ceremony for participants and their spouses because some 10,000 demonstrators rampaged through the streets setting fire to cars, stoning police officers, and smashing into businesses and looting them. The size and ferocity of the mob, which German police reported were bused to the demonstration from across Germany and even farther, caused overwhelmed police forces to keep Mrs. Trump from traveling to the G20 event.

By the end of the first day's melee, more than 130 police had been injured by the demonstrators and had called for reinforcements from law enforcement and military units across Germany. As usual, Greenpeace agitators were involved. "Hardcore anarchists" well-known to police, labeled the demonstration "Welcome to Hell." Well, they should know.

This is not the first G20 meeting attacked by the left; but the far left is more cohesive in Western Europe, especially France and Germany. They can bring out the "bodies," and the bodies are experienced in fighting law enforcement. Demonstrators in Hamburg used lasers to attack the eyes of police helicopter pilots. The *Guardian* referred, however, to "masked anti-capitalist protesters" who "torched cars and smashed shop windows…"

Apparently, the demonstrators also are experienced at securing financial support. German police reported that store owners had been approached, before the demonstrations, by individuals who said that, for a price, they could ensure that demonstrators would not smash and loot their stores.

In Europe and America, where freedom of speech, freedom of press, freedom of assembly, and free elections are taken for granted—and the most virulent, irresponsible, and obscene attacks on government are tolerated--there is no remotely conceivable justification for violent protest. Opponents of governments are free to express and promulgate their ideas and, for the most part, are welcomed by the media. If their goal were persuasion, they would not be in the streets burning cars, stoning police officers, and looting stores.

They operate on the revenant Marxist premise that the ruling class will defend their hegemony by any means, succumbing only to violence. This view, dating from a time when nations were ruled by kings and emperors and czars, has lost any conceivable relevance, today. (It never had any moral validity because Marx proposed replacing authoritarian regimes with dictatorships of workers.) The European leftists, today, are anachronisms in a "tradition" as dogmatic as fundamentalist Islamism. Perhaps that is why President Trump referred in Warsaw to "past" enemies of Western civilization—Soviet Socialism and National Socialism (Nazism)--at the same time he referred to the new threat from Islam.

To understand the old-left Marxian protestors in Hamburg, who have abandoned any serious argument and always foment violence as did their predecessors, and to understand the Postmodern professors, journalists, and other professional intellectuals in America who sought to stop Trump at any cost, is to trace the evolution of *philosophical collectivism*. It is progress from German Idealism and the anti-Enlightenment through its manifestations in Marxism and National Socialism—now utterly discredited with the exposure of German National Socialism in WWII and the collapse of Soviet Socialism in the late 20th Century—to the movement toward "cultural Marxism" after WWII==to today's philosophical manifestation of collectivism in Postmodern ideology.

Donald Trump is not a philosophical man, to say the least; he does not speak in terms of fundamental political principles. And yet, he ignited with his announcement that he would seek the nomination an opposition that sought to portray him as a barbarian tribal enemy of an entire inventory of collectives: racist, xenophobic, sexist, and misogynist. The charges expose the primitive level of political discourse of Postmodernism. There are no consistent principles, no coherent ideas, because Postmodernism does not believe in them. The only political reality is "identity" and division of Americans into the "exploiters" and the "exploited." This is how Postmodernism dissolves reason, individualism, principled political discourse, and the rule of law so that we are left with the screaming, rock-throwing, arsonist, looting mobs in the streets of Hamburg—or Baltimore.

The American "sense of life"

After more than a year of watching Donald Trump, I see nothing that could rationally justify the defensiveness, outrage, opposition verging on hysteria, and outright violence of his enemies. There is a "Trump or Us" mindset that suggests some deadly threat. Today, that response could be evoked only by a perceived threat to Postmodernism itself.

This threat is what, with no conscious intent, Donald Trump came to represent. The threat is what Ayn Rand characterized as the American "sense of life"—as America's emotional equivalent of Modernist philosophy—as "the best within us."

The election victory of Trump is an expression of a bewildered, battered, but still assertive American sense of life that values freedom, individualism, pride in achievement, and assertion of equality against any presumed "elite," values that are epitomized by the Declaration of Independence and preamble to the United States Constitution. That American spirit seized on Trump—the successful, proudly wealthy, "can do," "don't push me around" champion of last resort. That it was a last resort of the American sense of life, the Postmodernists agreed. The battle lines were drawn.

The danger is that President Trump seems to have little inkling on a philosophical level of what is a stake. The speech in Warsaw shows to me the hand of senior Trump advisor, Steven Bannon, who *does* understand in his own terms that a great clash of philosophical values is reaching its climax.

We cannot count on President Trump as more than a colorful, feisty avatar of the American sense of life. It will be wonderful if against all odds he prevails, as Ronald Reagan did, and temporarily interrupts American decline.

The last battle

The battle, however, will be fought within the walls of colleges, universities, and policy institutes. There is nowhere else that we come together, as a matter of course, to address explicit disagreements about the nature of reality, reason, man's nature and means of knowledge, the definition of human values, and the political system appropriate to the requirements of human existence.

At any given time, there are schools of thought that tend to dominate higher education. Their adherents resist challenges to their worldview. The philosophy called "Postmodernism" now dominates all departments of English and other literatures, philosophy, sociology, and anthropology, for example, but Postmodernism has deemed those disciplines marginal to the core of Postmodernism and so we have Black Studies, Latino Studies, Women's Studies, Gay and Lesbian Studies, and an infinity of specific courses on the politics, history, sociology, and philosophy of specific "identity" groups. An entire book could be written about the disintegration of traditional disciplines, which implied the possibility of a general knowledge and insight into a field, into disciplines "as seen" through the lens of racial, ethnic, sexual, and gender identity.

In other words, it may be anachronistic to envision universities and colleges and places where Postmodernism can be intellectually challenged. Because Postmodernism no longer recognizes the validity of intellectual arguments about the classic philosophical issues to which I have so often referred. Those questions about reason and individualism are nowhere on the agenda. "Reason" is now "rationale" the only relevant question is whose rationale for what power position?

It is deliciously tempting to make the argument that the arena of intellectual discussion is shifting to the social media. You can assert that Web sites, Facebook, and even Twitter seized the debate from the mainstream media—and their legion of talking heads from academia— and you will get no disagreement from the frustrated, baffled mainstream media.

It is another thing to expect that serious, sustained, and ultimately influential academic discourse on the internet will shift the tectonic plates of Modernism, Postmodernism, and whatever may be next. I would add into this mix, however, the remarkable ease of self-publishing on Amazon and other platforms, so that books and now whole libraries become available to readers without the say-so of the intellectual establishment. My parochial shire of Facebook features nonstop discussions of epistemology, neuroscience, metaethics, esthetics, and political economy, but that is atypical and thanks solely to the most influential non-academic, non-Establishment philosopher of our time, Ayn Rand, who mounted our era's most powerful challenge to Postmodernism on behalf of the American spirit.

Her works by now have delivered several generations of young intellectuals from the head-shrinking monopoly of Postmodernism. When American conservatives for the most part could not oppose postmodernism successfully because they opposed Postmodernist skepticism with religious faith, and when the great religious faiths could not oppose post-modernism because they espoused *premodernism*, Ayn Rand made entirely *secular* arguments for reason, science, individualism, egoism, and the limited constitutional republicanism that fosters capitalism, true liberalism, and gave rise to the benevolent humanistic spirit of America.

She was convinced, with good reason, I think, that the dominant philosophy of an era could be challenged successfully only in colleges and universities. She pointed out that a country's aspiring intellectuals go to college "shopping" for a philosophy—an integrated view of existence, knowledge, the nature of man, and the good—and rarely are open to changing that understanding in later life. I have seen nothing to challenge that view since her death in 1982.

Nor do I see how we can hope to contest Postmodernism in our universities. The upsurge of the American spirit that swept not only Trump but his party to power in 2016 was not of young Americans, who, according to polls, were the core electoral supporters of socialist Sen. Bernard Sanders. The constituency reached by Trump was not primarily a young, college-educated, rising generation. The Postmodernists in colleges are firmly in control of them. Postmodernists, when in power, do not tolerate disagreement, which they smear as bigotry or, at best, indication of the need for "re-education." Disagreements with Postmodernism are viewed as "insensitive," dangerous to students, racist, sexist or otherwise not worthy of discussion.

President Trump temporarily has won. We should enjoy what he accomplishes and discomfiture of his enemies. But in the longer perspective, Postmodernism has a strangle-hold on American intellectual life. You need only glance at our leading newspapers, opinion magazines, TV shows, and, yes, highly vocal Hollywood celebrities to perceive that dominance. Unless the American spirit reasserts itself explicitly, beginning in the colleges and universities, Postmodernist voices seem likely to have the last laugh.

For a new American Revolution

If there is hope, it is that increasingly, today, intellectual ferment has spilled out of academia. The impact of Ayn Rand typified how philosophical ideas with evident relevance to life, success, and happiness might reach enough adults—breaking through the "my life is about practical problems" mindset—to ignite an American "Great Awakening." Two such earthquakes have erupted in our history, both beckoning Americans back to their religious roots. Audiences of hundreds of thousands gathered in New England fields to hear the great leaders of these "awakenings." Nothing could block their resolve to renew the wellsprings of morality.

Characterizations of election eve 2016 hint at an improbable upsurge at the level of sense of life and political values, sweeping aside opposition and doubt, embracing hope.

That momentum can be sustained only by what Ayn Rand called "the new intellectual," the man or woman from any walk of life who accepts responsibility for thinking independently—and by doing so, leads. It is the supreme "populist" victory when Plato's "philosopher kings" cease to dominate an elite academic realm and walk among us.

If they do, then the hour of Thomas Jefferson and the new American Revolution will have come. Jefferson wrote: "I have sworn upon the altar of God eternal hostility against every form tyranny over the mind of man."

Sworn upon what any man holds sacred, this is the declaration of independence of reason.

Thanks

I wrote *Donald Trump and His Enemies* contemporaneously with the 2016 Presidential nominations, election, inauguration, and early months of the new Trump administration. The articles were published in "The Savvy Street," an online publication begun and ably edited by Vinay Kolhatkar, and on the Atlas Society Web site, where editor, David Kelley, and CEO, Jennifer Grossman, added insight and accuracy.

Editing at the line level all the way to the most discerning perspective was promptly and thoroughly completed by Donna Paris.

Strategic recommendations so vital to this kind of "written on the battlefield" book" were from Donna Paris and Dee Slavutin.

I relied throughout this book on the redoubtable scholarship of Professor Stephen R. C. Hicks in his 2004 book, *Explaining Postmodernism: Skepticism and Socialism from Rousseau to Foucault.* His subsequent lectures and articles on his blog and other Web sites, including *The Savvy Street*, keep affirming his importance for understanding the contemporary impact of Postmodernism.

It remains only to thank the online readers who, over almost a year, as these chapters were published, offered their affirmations, challenges, and suggestions—shaping this book from all sides of the historic clash of ideas that is an American election. I will risk mentioning among many Rick Koontz, Sally Jane Driscoll, Laurie Dow, Lisa Beggs, John Enright, Marsha Enright, Robert Malcolm, Anoop Verma, Kaila Halling, Dale Halling, Michael Hurd, Logan Darrow, John Kenny, Steve Horwitz, and Mike Renzulli.

On the honor roll of Facebook intellectuals who have used the medium for serious intellectual and esthetic investigations, these are awarded *summa cum laude*. I allude many times in my book to the charges leveled by the mainstream media against the upstart social media. There are reasons for complaint; genuine freedom always will be abused, by some, used to heroic effect by others.

But the internet—online news sites like the remarkable *Breitbart*, social media platforms like Facebook and Twitter, and myriad specialized sites of sometimes astonishing quality and integrity—challenged the dominance of mainstream reporting and interpretation and shaped the 2016 election. In truth, the populist media seized the initiative from the old liberal-left rainmakers of American elections and the decision went against the establishment. The defeat was bitter not least because the mainstream media, in response to the Trump challenge, progressively discarded neutrality, perspective, objectivity, and, in the end, even fairness and decency, to have their way—and they lost. We see now in the same media a new national campaign: to eject President Trump and reverse the verdict of the 2016 election.

The individuals named here, and hundreds of thousands of others—not by any means all Trump supporters, many were #neverTrump— conducted the democratic dialogue outside the mainstream media. In my own Facebook village, the level of discourse surpassed even the elite media in keeping the argument on the level of principles and facts. I am proud, most of all, that by the end of the scrap, there was a widespread agreement to avoid invective, emotional appeals, the *ad hominem* fallacy, the "argument from intimidation," and excessive huffing and puffing of all kinds.

We had been informed, somewhere along the line, in school, I suppose, that that is the discipline demanded by a search for truth. We once supposed that the elite of American journalism exemplified that discipline. Our faith—whatever remained of it--was a casualty of the election. I followed the *New York Times* editorial and columnist pages and soon lost track of the fouls committed.

American journalism had succumbed to Postmodernism. It was no use sighing that reporters and editorialists are "only human." On a given day, you could count half-a-dozen page-one leads to editorial matter with smarmy "all of us hate Trump" titles. Check it out; the record is there.

On the same days, there were posters, informed and intellectually acute, who filed their own stories of the election, candidates, and issues. As the target of the mainstream media became defeat of Donald Trump at any cost—with nonstop sensationalist sagas of political incorrectness dominating coverage—the social media shifted to the defense—and counter-attack

Every voter has a right to an opinion and choice. Does the media of a great democratic republic have a right to slant facts, photos, and commentaries—and devote every issue and every show--to defeat of a candidate? Of course, and it is right in doing so if the candidate is Adolf Hitler. But oh, beware of the cost of crying wolf! The media and its commentators constantly made probing attempts to get away with the portraying the election in those terms—and still is testing.

Who needed it? Serious discussion shifted to Facebook, Linked-in, and Twitter, where the 70-year-old Donald Trump was mastering the "new generation's media" to bypass the mainstream media to reach the American people with his message. That message might be welcome or despised, but on Twitter it was Trump's message as he wrote it.

Along with the "populist" uprising across the social media, it made the difference.

About the Author

In 1998, famous *New York Times* political columnist and expert commentator on language, William Safire, then also a Dana Foundation trustee, tapped Walter Donway to create and edit *Cerebrum: The Dana Forum on Brain Science*—now in its 19th year. Safire explained to the Foundation's financial vice president, Burton Mirksy, "He's a wordsmith." And then, in typical Safire fashion, cracked, "And he's also a Right-winger!"

The moment, and the comment, captured a great deal about Donway, and, of course, left out still more. He had been active in political campaigns as a citizen, and as a writer, since 1964, when he worked as an organizer for Republican candidate, Barry Goldwater, during his sophomore year at Brown University. In campaigns after that, he never was as enthusiastic—and sometimes didn't even bother to vote.

Far more than a "Right-winger," he was an genuine intellectual drawn to the powerful philosophical revolution launched by Ayn Rand with her novel, *Atlas Shrugged*, and a dozen books on epistemology (the theory of knowledge), ethics, politics, and esthetics that followed until her death in 1982. Her philosophy of "Objectivism," primarily a historic defense of reason, individualism, and laissez faire capitalism, brought into existence the modern libertarian movement and Libertarian Party politics. Rand herself had no patience with any libertarian politics not rooted in the fundamentals of philosophy, including the relationship between reason, inalienable individual rights, and capitalism.

Few Presidential candidates of any party met Rand's stern test of an advocacy of capitalism rooted in reason and individual rights. And yet, against the outright socialist, redistributionist, egalitarian-hippie politics of Sen. George McGovern, the 1972 Democratic Presidential candidate, she threw her support behind Richard Nixon—a clear-eyed calculated choice among available options. Donway ("rather dutifully," he says) became involved in the Nixon campaign in 1968 and again in 1972. Looking back, he comments: "This was Boston during the anti-war movement and student rebellion—the

Black Liberation Army and middle-class New Left kids were gunning down bank guards. So, when I held up my Nixon poster, guys came over, grabbed my collar, and wanted to fight."

Much later, his support of Nixon, which Donway saw as minor in is life, became the basis of bonding with Safire, who worked for Nixon in both campaigns, became chief Nixon speech writer along with Patrick Buchanan, and, as he commented later, "Managed to stay out of jail." He did more than that, becoming the showcase Libertarian among *New York Times* columnists—but soon an indispensable voice in politics and, in his "On Language" column in the Sunday *Magazine,* the country's best-known language "maven"—his favored term for it.

By then, Donway had published dozens of articles and essays for publications receptive to the libertarian point of view, including as a columnist for *Private Practice,* journal of the Congress of County Medical Societies, and *Human Events,* the renowned feisty Washington, D.C., weekly paper of conservative opinion edited by Tom Winters. At that time, *Human Events* was almost alone on the media scene as a critic of liberal-leftism and advocate of capitalism. At the same time, though, he published the lead op-ed article in *Wall Street Journal* "In Defense of Decades of Greed," solicited by *WSJ* editorial page editor, Robert Bartley.

When accused of "not looking at the other side," Donway laughs and points out that all his professional positions, as an executive at Brown University, the Commonwealth Fund (the country's earliest major foundation devoted to experimentation with health care programs and medical education), and the Dana Foundation were with "certified East Coast Liberal institutions." He says, "from 1969 until my retirement in 2004, I was a fixture of the Liberal-Left intellectual bureaucracy. Don't tell me I need to be exposed to that viewpoint!"

In effect, however, he found nothing to refute—or even seriously challenge—the philosophy of Objectivism. The real reform that called to him was of Objectivism itself, which had become cultish, intolerant, and closed to change. It was not unusual—closer to typical—for a powerful new philosophy that set itself against the verities, assumptions, and dogmas of its time. In 1990, David Kelley solicited Donway as one of the first trustees of the new "Institute of Objectivist Studies"—today, the Atlas Society, which states its mission as "Open Objectivism." For some two decades, he helped to set the philosophical direction of the organization, editing its first publication and contributing dozens of articles and lectures on every aspect of the philosophy and its application to contemporary questions.

Turning to full-time writing in 2004, when he retired as editor of *Cerebrum*, he created the publishing imprint, Romantic Revolution Books, recognizing Ayn Rand's powerful case for the nature of art and its importance to man's life. He has written and published four novels, three books of poetry, and two full-length memoirs under that imprint. His most recent book, *Not Half Free: The Myth that America is Capitalist*, charted the steep decline in American economic freedom beginning with the financial panic and stock-market crash of 2007-2009.

With the surprise candidacy of Donald Trump for the 2016 Republican Presidential nomination, Donway brought to bear his intellectual standards and lifetime experience with judging candidates according to philosophical libertarian standards. Beginning with skepticism—in fact, plain lack of interest—he came to view Trump as the imperfect, at times rough-hewn, American leader that a desperate American electorate had chosen as their champion against a self-perpetuating Washington bureaucracy and Congress, an increasing liberal-left interventionist-welfare state, and a cultural and intellectual establishment that measured America against Postmodernist philosophical skepticism, cultural Marxist, and identity politics--and found America's founding philosophy and values of today's American middle class contemptible. He came to view the election more as a choice between Trump and his enemies than a choice between Trump and Clinton—and so the title of this book.

In *Donald Trump and His Enemies: How the Media Put Trump Office*, Donway /narrates in real time, with all the drama, conflict, and surprise of the 2016 election, how Trump's brazen, uncompromising candidacy, and his refusal to flinch at any attack on himself or his family, forced America intellectuals on the Left, but especially in the media, to expose their collectivist priorities, willingness to grasp any means to achieve their ends, and hatred for the "deplorables," who, in the end, despite it all, chose Trump as their standard-bearer.

All Donway's books are available on Amazon:
https://www.amazon.com/author/Walter-Donway/

www.ingramcontent.com/pod-product-compliance
Lightning Source LLC
Chambersburg PA
CBHW071351280526
45787CB00001B/283